MASTERING
GUERRILLA
MARKETING

Other books by Jay Conrad Levinson

The Most Important $1.00 Book Ever Written

Secrets of Successful Free-Lancing

San Francisco: An Unusual Guide to Unusual
   Shopping (*with Pat Levinson and John Bear*)

Earning Money Without a Job

555 Ways to Earn Extra Money

150 Secrets of Successful Weight Loss
      (*with Michael Lavin and Michael Rokeach*)

Quit Your Job!

An Earthling's Guide to Satellite TV

Guerrilla Marketing

Guerrilla Marketing Attack

The Investor's Guide to the Photovoltaic Industry

Guerrilla Marketing Weapons

The 90-Minute Hour

Guerrilla Financing
      (*with Bruce Jan Blechman*)

Guerrilla Selling
      (*with Bill Gallagher and Orvel Ray Wilson*)

Guerrilla Marketing Excellence

Guerrilla Advertising

Guerrilla Marketing Handbook
      (*with Seth Godin*)

Guerrilla Marketing Online
      (*with Charles Rubin*)

Guerrilla Marketing for the Home-Based Business
      (*with Seth Godin*)

Guerrilla Marketing Online Weapons
      (*with Charles Rubin*)

The Way of the Guerrilla

Guerrilla Trade-Show Selling
      (*with Mark S. A. Smith and Orvel Ray Wilson*)

Get What You Deserve: How to Guerrilla-Market
   Yourself (*with Seth Godin*)

Guerrilla Marketing with Technology

Guerrilla Teleselling
      (*with Mark S. A. Smith and Orvel Ray Wilson*)

Guerrilla Negotiating
      (*with Mark S. A. Smith and Orvel Ray Wilson*)

MASTERING
GUERRILLA
MARKETING

100 Profit-Producing Insights
You Can Take to the Bank

Jay Conrad Levinson

Houghton Mifflin Company

Boston • *New York*

1999

For information about permission to reproduce selections
from this book, write to Permissions,
Houghton Mifflin Company, 215 Park Avenue South,
New York, New York 10003.

Library of Congress Cataloging-in-Publication Data

Levinson, Jay Conrad.
Mastering guerrilla marketing : 100 profit-producing
insights you can take to the bank / Jay Conrad Levinson.
p.   cm.
ISBN 0-395-90875-2
1. Marketing.   I. Title.
HF5415.L4796 1999
658.8 — dc21   99-33627   CIP

Printed in the United States of America

Book design by Robert Overholtzer

QUM 10 9 8 7 6 5 4 3 2 1

CONTENTS

INTRODUCTION

Many small businesses are run by people who don't know and don't want to know about marketing. Others are run by people who want to learn about marketing and who put its principles into practice. Still other small businesses are run by guerrilla marketers — those who strive to make the most of their marketing investments. Because these guerrillas take marketing seriously and are aware of its startling capability, I want to provide them with the necessary insights to master the process of marketing. Because so many companies struggle with their marketing plans rather than luxuriating in their power, then fall by the wayside simply because of a void in their marketing acumen, I want to guide business owners in mastering the guerrilla marketing process.

Much of what I say in my live marketing presentations is new, so fresh that it doesn't make it into the pages of any of my books. Nuggets of marketing astuteness fall into the cracks, regardless of their importance. All of them have been mined from those cracks and now appear in the pages of this book. In previous books, I attempted to give small business owners a grasp of marketing, a clear vision of what it can and cannot do, how to use it and not abuse it, how to have realistic expectations as to what all the media can do for you. In this book, I give business owners specific marketing insights to help them actually master the process, transforming their mastery into honest-to-goodness profits — large and consistent.

I can't think of anyone who types faster than I do. But marketing is changing much faster than I can type. Every day I learn of marketing tactics and practices that can make the difference between success and failure to guerrillas, and these pages are alive with state-of-the-moment marketing insights. And as marketing will continue to change as part of its nature, a book can only capture the essence of marketing for a fleeting instant. The information on these pages will change with time; the insights were selected for their timelessness. Most of them will still be true in 2100.

Rather than cover a wide range of marketing topics — and the range is endless — this book delves deeply into marketing's eleven most critical areas: planning, weaponry, media, online marketing, direct response, people, attitudes, technology, economizing, creativity, and action. Guerrillas should not be handicapped in those arenas.

Because of the many variables in marketing and the rapid changes in the marketplace, planning is more crucial than ever. Only companies with proper goals and plans will be able to negotiate the future with a clear view. The weaponry of marketing has undergone a dramatic alteration — such technology as cell phones, pagers, laptops, PDAs, and computer networking were light years from the mainstream when I wrote the first guerrilla marketing books. Today there are more weapons than ever, and there's a new electronic battleground in which they must be fired with consummate accuracy. Only those with the right insights will know how to hit bull's-eyes.

The media available to guerrillas is more fragmented than it ever has been, and it's going to break into even smaller pieces, all grand news to guerrillas who choose precious marketing over mass marketing every time. There is a broad array of weaponry available for guerrilla arsenals, and online marketing now plays a tremendous role in the arsenal. However, there is much more to online marketing than being online and having a Web site. Brand-new insights in this book explain to small businesses how to tower above huge competitors in cyberspace. My past three books addressed online marketing, and here I provide many more insights to lead you into the new marketing multiplex.

Direct response describes the direction in which marketing and commerce is heading. Rather than shouting vague messages to vague audiences, marketers are whispering just the right words in just the right ears, evoking the exact response they desire. These guerrillas understand that interactivity is at the heart of direct response and the Internet is the best direct-response technique in the history of free enterprise. It's hard to imagine that the World Wide Web did not exist when the first guerrilla marketing book was written. If you think guerrilla marketing thrives offline, wait till you see how it can soar online.

It is difficult to master marketing without a vivid understanding of how people relate to marketing and how marketing relates to people. Insight into human behavior is mandatory for marketers. People cherish their time now more than ever and yet are interrupted by intrusive marketing now more than ever. There are ways around the situation, but you must know how people think of marketing if you're not to be stopped in your tracks.

Obstacles beyond belief will leap up in your path, but guerrillas surmount these obstacles with aplomb because they are fueled with the attitudes possessed by those who seem to win every race they enter. Often, they are born with those attitudes. Frequently, they have to develop them, hone them, spread them throughout their organizations. Investigating these attitudes is really where marketing all begins — within the head of the marketer.

If you have insight into technology, you have x-ray vision of the potential of your company. Technology can help your business do more, satisfy more customers, profit more, and get you to the end of your rainbow more rapidly. Although it is constantly changing, technology can be viewed from a new perspective with insights that are not changing.

Guerrillas are able to economize because they are skilled in the art of not wasting money, rather than skimping on the use of it. Many business owners must make only a few tweaks in their marketing plans to move the business from red to black. So insights are provided to help them accomplish what astute guerrillas know by heart — frugality without the appearance of frugality.

Insights into creativity are more necessary than ever — simply because marketing creativity has gone awry, headed in the wrong direction with other marketing lemmings following it right off the cliff and into a sea of wasted marketing investments. In past guerrilla books, I offered sage advice for exerting the ultimate in marketing creativity, but every day, on TV, in the newspaper, on signs, online, and in magazines, I see that more insights are necessary — and in a hurry.

You can have all the insights on the planet and still fail in your business if you don't take action with your marketing, if you don't put energy behind each insight. Insights lead to action, which leads to profits. Clear enough? Armed with insights, you can master the process and make it produce twice the results it used to produce for you, ten times the results it produces for your competitors.

My first guerrilla marketing books were written to take small business owners from marketing haze to marketing clarity. My next guerrilla marketing books were written to take them to marketing excellence. This book takes both guerrilla marketing and guerrillas themselves to a higher level, the mastery of a seemingly complex process. That process is undergoing changes now more monumental than any time in history. A proliferation of marketing on every front has diluted the effectiveness of all marketing, while making consumers wiser, more skeptical and more guarded when it comes to their precious time.

As the world moves online nearly as fast as it rotates in the sky, the Internet is playing an increasingly important role in business

MASTERING GUERRILLA MARKETING

and in life, forcing marketing to become more interactive than ever. And this is just the start.

Being online does not grant you automatic prowess in marketing online. But knowing how to master marketing is invaluable if you're to compete in the marketplace of tomorrow, the one that is sweeping over commerce today. Unless you can master marketing, it will be nearly impossible to master online marketing. By filling the crevices in marketing and replacing them with insights and information, this book adds to the guerrilla marketing body of wisdom. It borrows information from some past guerrilla books, but presents insights contained in none of them.

In no previous book did I reveal an obvious but overlooked observation about the Internet: *its essence is action, its promise is speed, its most fertile opportunities are in its interactivity*. Capitalizing on all three is the only way to mine the wealth of the free-spending online community. If $1.92 billion was invested in Internet advertising in 1998, somebody certainly knows something about it. Why not you?

So much new and exciting marketing information is speeding down the information highway that it's hard to know the nuggets from the nonsense. The nuggets are in this book. The nuggets will help you attain the goals you have set, thanks to their ability to harness marketing and bring it under your rein, set it in your direction, put it under your control, and enjoy the satisfaction that comes only to the master. Once you have that talent to master guerrilla marketing, there is no limit to what it can achieve for you.

CHAPTER ONE

THE BENEFITS OF MASTERING MARKETING

I f you had all the money that was wasted in marketing each year, you'd be richer than Bill Gates and Warren Buffet combined. You'd have an endless supply of income on a regular basis. And your earnings would increase each year because more money is wasted than invested in marketing each year.

A depressing amount of money that is invested should be saved or given to charity because it has no chance of paying off. The reason it is being tossed to the winds is because the people in charge of investing it have no clear perspective of what marketing really can and can't do.

They know the words, but not the music. They have a superficial knowledge of the process of marketing, but lack the enlightenment they really need.

So they spend their marketing funds foolishly, frittering it away on false expectations. In many cases, they're doomed before they even begin because they don't start out in the right direction, they're not armed with the right ammunition, and they have no plan of attack. The money they waste comes directly from their profits. They may bring in money from work that they do remarkably well, but because they don't do their marketing well, that work was in vain.

One of the secrets of success in business is to provide quality in what you offer. Another is to realize that excellence isn't as much a goal as a process. Still another secret is to market with the aggressiveness and acumen of the guerrilla. Most businesses — start-ups and tiny companies to established giant corporations — do a bang-up job with the first secret, even the second, then fall on their faces with the third.

That is why this book exists.

I wrote it to provide insights most business owners lack. I wrote it to fill in the gaps in many business owners' knowledge of marketing. I wrote it to increase your profitability because every day I witness embarrassingly bad marketing in newspapers, magazines, and my mailbox, on radio, television, and the Internet, on signs, billboards, and my telephone. And I know how much money is being wasted in the pursuit of the impossible by the unenlightened.

Guerrillas know it is advantageous to have foresight and insight, for both are valuable, though they are not the same. An old Chinese proverb reminds us, "If you have foresight, you're blessed, but if you have insight, you're a thousand times blessed."

This is a book of marketing insights. You wouldn't attempt to climb a mountain without insights into climbing. You'd never jump into the ocean unless you had already learned how to swim. A marketing strategy isn't something you make up as you go along — it's something you must have at the outset, or dire circumstances will result. And yet, many people in charge of marketing are totally clueless when they begin. They jump in without knowing what they're doing.

When you have honest insights into marketing, you're ready to begin marketing. Until then, hold back on it or expect the worst. When you've finished reading this book, you'll have the insights. You'll know how to climb high. You'll know how to swim in seas brimming with sharks. And your profits will reflect your clarity.

The better you understand marketing and are able to actually master marketing, the higher your profits will be. That's the insight into profits that you must possess. The more you know what marketing can and cannot do for you, the lovelier the number on your bottom line. That's the most obvious benefit of mastering marketing.

Enjoying your work and feeling confident, in control, on top of everything, living a life relatively free of stress, especially in the marketing arena — these are the less obvious, yet no less important, benefits of mastering the guerrilla form of marketing.

If you know all there is to know about planning and producing a brochure, but don't know how to disseminate it or connect it with other elements of your marketing program — or dare to think you can market your business with that brochure and nothing else — your situation is woeful indeed. And your business will lose more than it will gain from that brochure. As guerrillas know, a job that is done 99 percent satisfactorily is a job done poorly — and marketing is just too expensive to do poorly. Guerrillas know well the difference between doing a project right the first time and having to redo it.

Most marketing these days is being done poorly. It looks a whole lot better than it produces. It is oriented to awards more than sales, to tradition more than reality, to the advertiser's ego more than the prospect's ego. It strives for hipness over aptness and aims primarily for laughs, razzle-dazzle, and cleverness rather than for profits . . . and it hits the bull's-eye for laughs, razzle-dazzle, and cleverness while missing entirely the target for profits.

Very often marketing campaigns are aimed directly at the profit bull's-eye, but they stop short of the target. A terrific mailing without a follow-up stops short. A telemarketing campaign without a stage-setting ad campaign or mailing stops short. An ad that does not fit cohesively with other marketing stops short. And any marketing that commences without a plan of attack stops short before it even has a chance to establish momentum.

Television advertising provides us with some of the most brilliant, exciting, stimulating, and fascinating mini-films we've ever seen. As such, they're enthralling to watch. But as commercials, which is what they are supposed to be, they are positively dismal, even appalling. They focus on almost everything except the product. In fact, many times, it's not even mentioned till the very end. This lack of insight is to be blamed on witless people who worship at the shrines of entertainment, special effects, humor, and celebrity instead of those who concentrate on profits, sales, motivation, and relationships.

When people see your marketing, they're supposed to say, "Wow! I want that product!" They're not supposed to say, "Wow! What a great film!"

An instructor at the Harvard Business School says that there have been four ages of global economic activity. He said that the first age was agricultural, the second was industrial, the third was information, and the fourth, which we've just entered, is the age of creativity. It is? Where can I find proof? Not in marketing, that's for sure. Guerrillas define creativity in marketing as something that increases profits. There is a notable lack of creativity by that definition in most marketing campaigns.

Millions — no, make that billions — of dollars each year are wasted by being invested in marketing that makes the writer, art director, and producer feel good, while the accountant reaches into his drawer for another hit of Tums.

These days, television viewers, after watching a commercial, often ask:

- "Whose commercial is this? I just can't tell."
- "That sure was a great commercial! Who was it for?"
- "Boy! Dennis Rodman is terrific! What was he plugging in that spot?"
- "Fabulous commercial! Was that for Nike, Bud, Pepsi, or Guess jeans?"
- "Did you catch the name of that advertiser? I sneezed and missed it."

When I was toiling in advertising agencies, which I did for a dozen years, I was taught that if you have 30 seconds to sell a product, you should use all 30. These days, the lesson seems to be that if you have 30 seconds to sell a product, use the last three seconds to sell it and the first 27 to be sparkling and attention-getting.

Admakers seem to do all in their power to call attention to their ad when they should be calling attention to their product or service. The idea is to forget the marketing and make the product or service interesting. If you don't do that, you lack the insight that true creativity in marketing generates profits.

Web sites are guilty of the same crime. Many are creative in an artistic sense, yet devoid of creativity in the profitability sense. Same for many magazine ads and radio commercials. Same for a lot of direct mail. Why do you suppose people call it "junk mail"?

Guerrillas let prospects know right off the bat who is doing the marketing. They are not self-conscious that it is marketing and do not try to disguise marketing as pseudo-entertainment. They don't kid themselves by thinking, "If I'm clever enough, people will never guess that this is a commercial." They are not disgusted by the idea of showing their name onscreen throughout the commercial or using their name in a headline. They do not try to fool the public with their shifty moves and special effects. They are not adverse to repeating their main message once or twice. They are not embarrassed to present the benefits that their product offers. And they realize that marketing can do a whole lot more than generate awareness.

To help people find their way through the maze of superinformation, guerrilla creativity is more necessary than ever. It's necessary to help prospects know who you are, how your offering will make their lives better, why they should buy what you offer immediately. It is crucial to create a desire to buy what you're selling, to break through the clutter of inane marketing.

In a sense, this makes marketing a more fertile ground for guerrillas than at any other time in history. The competition is looking the other way — at awards judges, at their peers, at their own artistic souls. They are not looking directly into the eyes, hearts, and minds of their prospects. If you do, you'll be noticed. Even better, you'll be profitable.

The trend in current marketing? *More of the same.* That means more misguided, ill-advised, poorly planned, unrealistic, self-congratulating, silly, beside-the-point propaganda that generates profits for advertising agencies and marketing consultants, but not for the people signing the checks that pay for this kind of marketing. It is the result of lacking insight at the outset. And that's like diving into a swimming pool that has no water.

Guerrilla marketing has developed and flourished as a result. Where the first guerrilla marketing books were written for small businesses with limited capital, they are now embraced by large multinational corporations that are sick and tired of tossing money away.

Marketing of the guerrilla variety differs from marketing of the traditional variety in fifteen crucial ways. Each way seems to favor small business. These are fifteen hallmarks of guerrilla marketing.

1. It requires that you invest time, energy, and imagination in the marketing process rather than investing only money.
2. It is based on psychology — laws of human behavior — more than on guesswork and judgment.
3. It uses profits as the only yardstick for measuring its performance.
4. It is geared to small business and cognizant that many large businesses are only big small businesses.
5. It encourages marketers to use the gifts bestowed by today's simple-to-use technology and advises anyone with technophobia to see a technoshrink.
6. It removes the mystique from marketing and enables practitio-

ners to gain insight into the entire marketing process rather than being intimidated by it.

7. It changes the focus of marketing from competition to cooperation, asking guerrillas to see who they can help and who can help them instead of who they can obliterate. The driving force: the good of the customer.

8. It suggests that marketers aim for relationships rather than single sales, keeping score by the number of relationships more than by sales tallies.

9. It suggests that advertising alone does not work, direct mail alone does not work, public relations alone does not work, and a Web site alone doesn't work — that only marketing combinations, such as advertising, direct mail, public relations, and a Web site, work.

10. It counsels guerrillas to direct their gaze not at diversification and expansion as much as at focusing and intensifying their niche. When companies lose focus, they are in for grim times ahead.

11. It suggests that guerrillas grow their businesses geometrically with fervent follow-up and reliance upon the enormous referral power of customers, rather than by growing linearly by constantly adding new customers. Guerrillas aim first and foremost not at obtaining new customers but at nurturing and following up existing customers, as it costs one-sixth as much to sell something to an existing customer than to sell the same thing to a new customer.

12. It is oriented to giving as much taking, providing free information, tips, gifts, and consulting to prospects and customers. Guerrillas make generosity part of their overall marketing plan and continually think of things they can give to rather than take from people. This mindset opens wide the conduits through which profits flow.

13. It is concerned primarily not with the large but with the small — single individuals, small businesses, and minor details.

Guerrillas achieve more pinpoint accuracy than traditional marketers, whose primary concern is groups — who aim for the target more than the bull's-eye.

14. It is completely planned and always intentional. Nothing occurs due to happenstance or accident; guerrillas know that everything they do and say is marketing, so all of it is on purpose.
15. It provides one hundred weapons for guerrillas to use when marketing, fifty of those weapons being free. With so many free weapons, guerrillas utilize as many as they can.

Most important, trends in current marketing require guerrillas to succeed in an increasingly competitive marketplace. Marketing of the guerrilla variety allows guerrillas to feel the sensation of being in complete control of marketing rather than the other way around. With these insights, guerrillas do not waste money and are not forced to downsize or enter the bankruptcy courts.

In these pages, you are provided with the insights to actually master not only marketing itself, but guerrilla marketing as well. That's the kind that is helping small — and enormous — businesses in every corner of the earth.

Is it a coincidence that Microsoft is an enormously profitable company while engaging in extremely insightful marketing? I don't think so. It's because Microsoft worked hard to get where it is and doesn't want to lose its hard-earned money on marketing that fires blanks. Neither do I. Neither do you. Neither does any self-respecting guerrilla.

CHAPTER TWO

INSIGHTS INTO PLANNING

1

The first insight of all is that guerrillas *plan backward,* beginning with the attainment of their loftiest goals in the future, then work to the present. If you can allow yourself to visualize success, the path to it will be easier to find. Most companies see the beginning of the path in front of them, but don't see where it leads in the distance. Their short-sightedness gets them in trouble when change or unforeseen circumstances occur. It even impairs their ability to function when confronted with success.

The hardest job in the planning of marketing is *seeing the target.* You must remove the shackles of insecurity and fear in order to travel to your final destination. So you've got to think as though you've been attaining your goals all along as you plan for your distant future. You must see the company at its finest in twenty years in order for it to operate at its peak in ten years. By knowing what must be accomplished for such optimum performance, you can see where you must be in five years. That helps you concentrate on what must be done by the end of one year. And that points the way to what you've got to do tomorrow, to do today, to do now. When the golf ball is in the middle of the fairway and the green is two hundred yards away, the great golfers don't aim for the green. They aim for the cup.

You must know exactly where the cup is. Knowing where the

green is won't cut it for you. Knowing that the fairway is in front of you won't do it either. Most small businesses are run by owners who stand at the tee, club in hand, but aren't really certain in which direction they should aim. They can hit the ball, possibly even hit it long. But that won't get the ball *into the cup,* where it belongs.

Guerrilla businesses operate with marketing plans that factor in success and growth, change and flexibility. These plans shine a bright light far ahead, illuminating a target that exists only in the mind of the owner. That owner must put that same target into the minds of those who work with him or her — employees and co-workers, marketing partners and suppliers.

The way the business owner does it is with a plan that clearly shows the path upon which he or she is traveling and the destination to which it leads. It helps in all decision-making — from advertising to personnel. It has room for expansion, diversification, and success. Although it enables the business to operate in the here and now, it keeps a sharp focus on the there and then.

2

Although the soul of planning exists within the mind of the planner, the heart resides in the research he or she does. Knowledge gained from research will provide stability and reality to a plan. It will guide the hopes and ambitions of the planner while pointing to goals and tactics. The research must temper both boldness and timidity at the same time with the radiant glow of information.

The guerrilla possesses the insight to *begin planning with research.* The more concrete the research, the more sensible the plan. Plans gain strength as guerrillas gain wisdom in the following areas.

- **Product or service:** Guerrillas learn what makes it different, better, desirable. They find ways to improve it and add value to it.
- **Benefits:** Research into the benefits offered by the product should be reflected in the marketing plan, especially benefits not offered by others.
- **Market:** Plans exist not in a vacuum but in relationship to an entire marketplace. Guerrillas become experts in their market before planning.
- **Industry:** Guerrillas want to see their industry as a whole to help

them spot vulnerabilities and opportunities, to learn from successes and failures.

- **Competition:** Sane marketing plans are created according to dreams adjusted to competitive activity. Guerrillas are rarely taken by surprise.
- **Customers:** Rich sources of guerrilla data are customers of guerrillas and customers of competitors of guerrillas. Research mines these sources
- **Prospects:** Savvy marketing plans specify who the prospects are because research identified and located them before the plan was created.
- **Media:** Guerrillas learn the best ways to reach their target prospects and incorporate what they've learned about the media in their marketing plan.
- **Internet:** It's so simple to scour cyberspace for marketing intelligence that all guerrillas consider cyber-searching mandatory before planning.
- **Technology:** Because speed and efficiency can spur effective marketing, guerrillas look into how technology can propel them to their goals.

The end result of research should be an arrow pointing in the right direction and a bow with the power to get the arrow to the target. The marketing plan is the quiver in which the bow and arrow are kept.

3

The primary purposes of a plan are to state a goal and to illustrate ways to achieve it. This simple insight will enable you to *create a plan that puts the goal into plain sight,* then directs you to it with minimal mumbo jumbo. The plan should actually begin with the goal so that everything else in the plan falls into place.

Perhaps your goal is a big number — $5 million in sales by the end of one year. It might be a small number — ten new clients by the end of one year. Maybe it's an attitude — to provide the best customer service in the history of your industry. It could be a promise — to deliver hot chicken meals within thirty minutes of receiving an order. Your goal might be a statement — to achieve a 30 percent share of market by December 31, 2002. Possibly it's a production target — to cut the defect rate to less than 1 percent. It could also be an expansion figure — five new outlets a year for the next five years. And, in our new age of work enlightenment, your goal may be oriented to lifestyle — to consistently raise profits by 15 percent annually while working from home four days a week.

Guerrillas realize that they have a broad selection of goals and that they may choose to have more than one goal. They know that the more specific they are about their goal, the easier it will be to visualize and attain. They are very careful never to burden themselves with too many goals, for each may be sacrificed in pursuit of the others. They set goals for the near and distant future. The longer into the distant future they can project, the more specific they can be about the near future. Guerrilla goals take the inevitability of change into account. They factor in the changes that will occur in the market, in the economy, in the currency, in technology, and in the guerrilla personally.

One of the first steps the guerrilla must take is to define the goal of the marketing plan. The guerrilla wants to ensure that everyone connected with the company understands why the organization exists in the first place. The guerrilla's goal must be measurable so that he or she can gauge performance against it. It is quantifiable. It is out in the open.

The guerrilla wants to be able to show the marketing plan to everyone involved in the company so that they can focus on the marketing goals and clarify their own mission. The guerrilla has tangible goals that must be reached through a successful marketing plan, business plan, and production plan. The hallmark of these goals is realism.

Guerrillas set goals that can be met by creating an unmistakable path leading to them and benchmarks along the way to measure their progress.

4

O ne of the key insights into creating an ideal marketing plan is to *keep it brief.* This forces you to maintain an exceptionally clear focus on your goals. It prevents you from inserting unnecessary verbiage into your plan. It is a safeguard against rambling. And it enables those to whom you show your plan to read it and understand it before their eyes glaze over and they fall asleep.

Many marketing plans for potentially exciting companies are as long-winded as a politician's speech. They are filled with business jargon and language best reserved for legal briefs. They may have a point to them somewhere, but readers become lost on the way to it. Too many plans include information that belongs in business plans or world almanacs, but not in marketing strategies.

A tedious plan obscures the focus and obfuscates the targets. Instead of inspiring action, a tedious plan induces boredom. It's astonishing that the inability to be concise is the only thing denying many entrepreneurs success.

This seems to indicate that inherent in the ability to write a superlative marketing plan is the ability to write. If you get that notion, you're getting the right idea. To create a winning marketing plan, you've got to be able to write using simple sentences, simple phrases, simple words. You've got to use plain English, not fancy business jargon. You must get to the point. And you've got to write incisively enough to run your company by a plan that fits on one page.

An effective guerrilla marketing plan fits on only one page — in only one paragraph. It calls for a mere seven sentences. And only one of those sentences is a long one. The canniest of guerrillas are succinct enough to state their marketing plan in a mere seven words. "Goal: Video brochure requests from qualified prospects." It states the gist of the plan clearly, describing exactly what the marketing is supposed to do. The brevity makes it almost impossible to head in the wrong direction or select the wrong media. Marketing that is judged by brief strategies is easier to keep on target. Strategies exist to guide all marketing ideas, now and in the future. This is why guerrillas make the strategies succinct.

There may be hundreds of pages of documentation attached to the plan, with details of the target market and the media to be used to communicate with that market. But the actual plan is only seven sentences long. Every person who studies such a plan can *understand* it.

5

A marketing plan is going to be only as good as the people entrusted to breathe life into it. As all guerrillas know, action is the aim of the exercise. That means having the insight to know that *action is the purpose of planning.*

That's you I'm talking about when I mention action. Marketing is a three-way process. It involves employees or independent contractors or representatives of you. Marketing also involves customers: attracting customers is the purpose of the marketing plan. The third part of the process is the guerrilla. You are the impetus for action between the first two parts. You are the person who creates the marketing plan, then brings it to life. You direct those who create your marketing, you convince customers to accept your offer, you always follow up.

Unless you are a person who can motivate action, your plan will die on the drawing board. The equation for success is representatives, customers, and yourself. The rep's job is to create, produce, and activate the marketing. The customer's job is to respond to the marketing. Your job is to take action so that the right word gets out to the right people.

A plan that does not invite action is a plan lacking in an important element. It should clearly state what action is required and how to take that action. The person in charge of marketing must have an attitude that combines optimism with energy so that marketing tasks are handled with enthusiasm.

This attitude comes from a plan that inspires confidence, that begs for action to be taken. If small business owners do not have this attitude, they find someone within their organization who glows with the right attitude, who is bristling to take action, and who is 100 percent tuned in to the marketing plan. But guerrillas run their own marketing show, and a marketing plan without the right attitude and action backing it is like an automobile without a steering wheel and engine.

Guerrillas, having the right attitude, are willing to take the proper action, to serve as the steering and the power behind successful marketing plans. Without the steering and power, those marketing plans would be academic. Their purposes may have been lofty. They may have been crafted with clear language. Perhaps they were even cogent and brief. But without the vitality of a guerrilla calling the shots and making certain the plans sprouted wings, they would wither and die on the page.

6

The insight to recognize the difference between a marketing plan and a business plan is necessary if you want to have the best of each. *Marketing plans are part of business plans.* They focus on narrow areas related primarily to marketing. Unlike business plans, they don't cover important items such as management, financial projections, and inventory. Instead, they are intentionally limited in their scope. What areas do they cover?

The first sentence of the tight marketing plans created by true guerrillas spells out *the purpose of their marketing.* It's to solicit video brochure requests. Or to increase patient count to 50 per week. It's to generate 175 new leads each month. Or to generate store traffic of 1,500 people weekly. All the marketing is intended to achieve the purpose stated in the first sentence of the plan.

The second sentence dictates *the benefits or competitive advantages* they'll stress to achieve that purpose. The guerrilla does not pepper his or her marketing benefits, but instead selects the most unique, desirable, and believable of the benefits and stresses that one benefit — or two at most. Marketing may mention all the benefits, but it concentrates on the big guns, the guns lacking from the competitors' arsenals.

The third sentence of guerrilla marketing plans describes the *target audience.* Most guerrillas identify more than one target, so this sentence may list several audiences.

The fourth — the long sentence — lists the *marketing weapons* guerrillas will use to accomplish their goals. There are 100 weapons to choose from, and the guerrilla knows that the idea is to start with many, keep careful track, then narrow the weapons down to those proven in action.

The fifth sentence explains the guerrilla's *niche in the marketplace.* Guerrillas must carve out a position where they stand for something, and the marketing must reflect that distinctive positioning. It's stated in the marketing plan and apparent in every marketing weapon every used.

The sixth sentence puts the guerrilla's *identity* into a single statement. Guerrillas are careful to communicate their actual identity rather than some phony image. There's a big difference, and the difference is truth and honesty. Don't think customers don't know the difference, because they do.

The seventh sentence of a guerrilla marketing plan tells *the budget,* expressed as percentage of projected gross sales. Marketing plans limited to these seven topics tend to produce greater profits.

7

A s guerrillas have the good sense to begin with a plan, they are also blessed with the insight that the plan is your guide and you are the master. The idea is to create a plan that you can follow without strain and yet have the flexibility to veer from the plan when necessary.

An easy-to-implement plan should be reviewed every four to six weeks so you can hone your focus and reevaluate the plan in the light of a new month. Pray that you can stay with the plan without making changes to it. Every six months, be open to making alterations if absolutely necessary. But don't make changes to your plan unless you are forced to do so by market circumstances, technology advancements, or a new competitive onslaught.

The ideal situation is to stay with your marketing plan *forever.* This means you drafted a wise plan originally, one with built-in flexibility so that it didn't have to change as the world changed. The more common situation is to stay with your plan for one year, then make minor changes. The plan's purpose will probably stay the same. So will the primary benefit. But you may decide to focus on one instead of three target audiences. You probably will decide to eliminate 80 percent of the marketing weapons you're using because the other 20 percent are doing such a spectacular job. Your niche will remain the same. So, we hope, will your identity. And the percent you invest in marketing will probably go down as your sales rise. No reason to invest more in marketing just because you're successful. Just invest more wisely. You're in this for profits, not ego.

And, sure enough, there may be circumstances that cause you to change your marketing plan. The Internet may have grown so large so fast that you redirect your marketing to an online focus. You realize that your sales force is so good now that you should aim more for leads than for completed sales, knowing the salespeople can do the rest. An engineering breakthrough means you can make claims in the area of speed, claims you or your competition have never been able to make. A competitor begins offering his services for half the price you charge.

Drastic changes in situations merit drastic changes in marketing plans. Change whenever you must change. Stay the course at all other times. When must you change? If you have to ask the question, you probably shouldn't change one word of your marketing plan. Never make changes in response to the marketing tactics of others, but consider making them in response to the marketing strategies of others. The concept to embrace here is that you should feel *forced* to change your marketing plan by the realities of the market and not merely because you changed your mind. The best plans are those that are able to remain the same.

8

The biggest mistake in the area of planning is to fail to create a marketing plan at the outset. Use your guerrilla insight to *be sure it is oriented to the future as much as the present and to the present as much as the future.* Even though your plan is brief and simple, it should be your guiding force for the next decade. So you don't want it to begin with errors.

To protect yourself against mistakes at the outset, recognize that to create a marketing plan is to take a risk. I ask you to commit like crazy to your marketing purpose — the topic of your first sentence — as it's probably your commitment that's going to make the marketing successful. At the same time, I alert you to your ally, flexibility, which will allow you to refocus on the benefits you're heralding, to narrow the target audience so you can reach them more often. You need to be discriminating with your weapons so you know which ones have real firepower and which ones fire blanks. Add flexibility to your commitment so that your marketing plan is alive and vital no matter what the competitive situation. If you know what the pitfalls are when creating your marketing plan, you can avoid them. It is important that guerrillas adhere to the following five rules — they will lead to success.

- **Spare the details.** Put the details into the documentation that supports the plan, but not into the plan itself. Nobody needs readership and viewership figures in a marketing plan.
- **Avoid sloganeering.** A marketing plan is no place for an advertising theme or a headline. It does not need the touch of a copywriter or direct-mail writer. Write it with simple words and a matter-of-fact tone.
- **Don't lie.** Don't pin your hopes on a benefit that you don't actually offer. Consumers are smarter than ever these days and getting smarter. Don't select a target audience you can't afford to reach. Don't include weapons you probably won't use. Never fib about your identity.
- **Create a benchmark.** Some businesspeople create powerful plans but then fall prey to enticing marketing schemes that don't correspond to their plan. The plan is the benchmark by which you judge your marketing before it is made public.
- **Dare to dream.** The best marketing plans sound fictitious at first, but then become nonfiction. They include lofty goals that exist only in dreams today, with guideposts to transform them into reality tomorrow. They should be infused with hope and optimism.

9

The planning insight that can save you the most money is to have *realistic expectations*. It is depressing to consider how many splendid marketing plans were laid to waste by expectations that had no basis in reality. The biggest culprit in this area is false expectations about time.

The business owner drafts a plan, implements the plan, then goes into a state of acute blues because goals weren't met in a hurry. Sales are up. Traffic is up. Profits are up. But they're not up enough. Goals aren't being reached soon enough. Worse yet, the plan is only starting to take effect and the person in charge believes it should have taken full effect by now. What happens most of the time? The business owner drops the marketing plan and begins again. Yet the goals would have been met if the plan had been given *more time*. The business owner thought that following the plan should have brought more immediate results. The truth, according to guerrillas, is that you've got to do everything right and stick with the plan; be patient. And that's too long to wait for those in search of quick gratification.

Superb marketing does not provide results instantly: the process is more than an event. In most cases, it involves changing human behavior. And the process takes effect *gradually*. Even when products or services offer dramatic improvements, consumers embrace them in super-slow motion. This is due to human nature, not poor marketing. Many deserted marketing plans would have worked wonders had they been given the chance. But most business owners just don't give it the chance because they want it to work faster than it can work. And so it never works at all.

Realistic expectations involve the element of patience. Even if you set a goal that's larger than life, you can't shrink time to achieve your goal. Guerrillas expect slow and steady improvement in all areas. These expectations are boosted by the guerrilla's penchant for constant improvement by tightening the screws, attending to the details. Whoever said "God is in the details" demonstrated a superb grasp of reality.

Realistic expectations are not unambitious expectations. Or low expectations. They show an understanding that marketing is a lot like evolution — heading in the right direction, but at its own pace. We are reminded by ancients, "Don't push the river; it flows by itself."

Once you've created a winning marketing plan, give it the time to achieve victory, to flow toward your goals. Remember that its speed limits are different from yours.

10

Guerrillas always have the insight to *know what marketing is not.* They're pretty sure what marketing is. They're convinced by their real-life success in marketing battles that marketing is an opportunity for them to help their customers, a method to profit from their business, a chance to fuse and cooperate with other businesses in their community or industry, and a way to build lasting relationships.

They're well aware that marketing is a fancy word that means selling products and treating people well. Most important, they are not misled by marketing misconceptions. Here is what marketing is not.

- Marketing is not advertising. Don't think for a second that because you're advertising, you're marketing. There are more than one hundred weapons of marketing. Advertising is one of them. But there are ninety-nine others. If you are advertising, you are simply advertising — you are doing only 1 percent of what you can do.

- Marketing is not direct mail. Some companies think they can get all the business they need with direct mail. Mail order firms may be right about this. But most businesses need a plethora of other marketing weapons to support direct mail, to make direct mail succeed. If you are using direct mail only, you're no guerrilla.

- Marketing is not telemarketing. For business-to-business marketing, few weapons succeed as well as telemarketing — with scripts. You can dramatically improve your telemarketing response by augmenting it with advertising — yes, advertising — and direct mail — yes, direct mail. Marketing is not telemarketing alone.

- Marketing is not brochures. Many companies rush to produce a brochure about the benefits they offer, then pat themselves on the back for creating a quality brochure. Is that brochure really all there is to marketing? It's an important aspect of your plan when mixed with ten or fifteen other important parts — but all by itself? Forget it.

- Marketing does not mean advertising only in the Yellow Pages. Most, and I do mean most, companies in the U.S. run a Yellow Pages ad and figure that it takes care of their marketing. Advertising in the Yellow Pages only is sufficient for 5 percent of all businesses. For the other 95 percent, it's a disaster in the form of marketing ignorance. Use a Yellow Pages ad as part of your arsenal — but only as part.

- Marketing is not show business. There's no business like show business, and that includes marketing. Think of marketing as sell business, as create-a-desire business, as motivation business. Guerrillas aren't in the entertainment business — marketing is not meant to entertain.

- Marketing is not a stage for humor. If you use humor in your marketing, people will recall your funny joke, but not your compelling offer. If you use humor, your campaign will be funny the first and maybe the second time. After that, the humor will be grating and will hinder the very concept that makes marketing successful — repetition.

- Marketing is not an invitation to be clever. You don't want potential customers to remember the cleverness of your marketing

— it's your *offer* they should remember. Cleverness is a marketing vampire, sucking attention away from your offer.

- Marketing is not complicated. Guerrillas begin with a seven-sentence guerrilla marketing plan, then select from one hundred weapons, half of them free. Not too complicated.
- Marketing is not a miracle worker. More money has been wasted because marketers expected miracles than because of any other misconception. Expect miracles, get ulcers. Marketing is the best investment in America if you do it right, and doing it right requires planning and patience.

CHAPTER THREE

INSIGHTS INTO WEAPONRY

11

There are one hundred guerrilla marketing weapons. Guerrillas know that all these weapons are not created equal. Some have more potency than others, some have more pertinence, some make more economic sense. Of the one hundred weapons, ten are proving to be the cornerstone of successful marketing programs. Although all guerrillas do not use all ten weapons all the time, most guerrillas use most of the weapons most of the time. One of the most powerful weapons in your arsenal — your competitive advantage — may already exist. A *mandatory* weapon is your *competitive advantage.*

This is the foundation of your guerrilla marketing plan. It is the focal point of all your other marketing tools, the eye of your cyclone. Your competitive advantage is a benefit that is unique to your company. It is something that your prospects want, something they can't get elsewhere. It is what distinguishes you from your competition.

If you don't have an inherent competitive advantage, you must create one — a real one. The best competitive advantages — shining like diamonds from within the company's current modus operandi — are discovered by marketing geniuses. They are competitive edges that can be made to sound like Mt. Everest–sized edges. "Flame-broiled," says Burger King, visually and verbally, because their research has shown them that customers equate flame-broiled with health and good taste. "Your gas is free if we don't wash your windshield," says Dan's Auto Service, a local gas station that has created a competitive edge.

How do you create a competitive advantage that will serve as the cornerstone for all of your marketing? It should meet four criteria.

- **It is a positive benefit.** It is not one of your features, but one of the ways people gain by doing business with you. It's something they want.
- **Nobody else offers it.** Maybe they do offer it, but they don't talk about it so nobody knows it. The more unique and hard to copy, the better.
- **Your advantage can be stated simply.** Long-winded explanations aren't necessary to communicate your advantage. A few well-selected words are sufficient.
- **Your advantage can be communicated verbally and visually.** People know it's you when you say or show your competitive advantage in *any* medium.

Once you have yours nailed down, be sure that it sings out in all of your other marketing materials. Make it part of your identity. Make it part of your niche. It's the first thing you want prospects to think of when they read or hear your name.

12

Guerrillas know well that people want to do business with friends instead of strangers if at all possible. Guerrillas *dive into an ocean of friends through community involvement.* You become involved with the community by helping it. The community becomes involved with you by helping you.

Involvement in the community means more than joining clubs — it means contributing your brains and energy to the community. It means working hard to make your community a better place. You can prove your conscientiousness and noble efforts with the work you do instead of the words you say.

One of the keys to marketing — keeping it very personal, because the more personal the marketing the better — is to establish relationships through networking. From these relationships come business associates, marketing partners, investors, employees, customers, prospects, suppliers, and referrals. The community is one of the richest sources of networking opportunities. You serve on committees. You go to little league games. You help set up parades, holiday decorating programs, Thanksgiving Day turkey races, Fourth of July celebrations. People see you in action. They see that you're a person of action, a person who keeps his or her word. So when you say something in a marketing context, they tend to believe you. When you make an offer, they know it's not going to be bogus. You've proved yourself in the community.

There are wrong ways to demonstrate community involvement as well. If you volunteer to work on a committee but are never available for meetings, or if you sponsor a little league team and don't show up for games, you're proving yourself to be crass and superficial, simply using the community to get business instead of working for it for altruistic reasons. Consumers are more sophisticated than ever these days. People know the difference between serving the community and serving yourself. If you're not willing to devote honest time and energy to your community, you're better off forgetting this weapon and leaving it to the real guerrillas in your community. I hope for your sake that none are your direct competitors.

Your community is not merely defined by geography. Guerrillas become involved with their industrial community, though it may reach from coast to coast or across the ocean. Digital communities are springing up everywhere as the world goes online. Whatever the size or scope of your community, the guerrilla rule remains the same: do unto others as they hope you will do unto them. As part of the community, they are hoping for your help, not your hype.

13

Guerrillas are blessed with the insight that *the more you give, the more you get*. That's why they so eagerly become involved with the community, giving their energy and enthusiasm. Their love of giving opens wide the conduits through which the getting occurs. They are alert for things they can give away for free and are known for their generosity — with information, with expertise, with time, even with gifts.

Think of the kinds of things you might give away for free in your business. They could be pamphlets filled with tips that can help your prospects. Perhaps you can give free seminars or clinics on your area of expertise. You might offer free delivery, free installation, or free service for the first thirty days. Some gas stations offer free car washes; some restaurants offer free coffee refills; some video stores offer free rentals for an extra two or even three days.

People are unconsciously drawn to companies that offer items for free, and they are wary of those that are always in a mode of taking. Once you are focused on what you can *give*, your orientation becomes attuned to the customers' needs. You think in terms of keeping them satisfied, staying in touch with them, providing them with helpful knowledge with your newsletter — or your catalog. You think in terms of keeping them contented and they sense your positive attitude. They like you. They believe you. They trust you. Why not? You seem to have their wants on your mind, not your own.

Guerrilla companies use prospect and customer questionnaires to find out what their prospects and customers want and need. They are always on the alert for the latest in advertising specialties because they know that everybody loves free things and that many promotional gizmos are priced under a dime. If they want to beef up their response to an offer, they toss in a freebie for people who respond within thirty days — and the response shoots up like a rocketship.

In an age where information is king, guerrillas recognize the value of information and the economy of disseminating it. They regale their prospects with free data in the form of seminars, videos, audiotapes, fliers, booklets, computer disks, and online offerings of a myriad varieties. The more creative they can become in their generosity, the better likelihood they'll see it reflected in their profitability.

As your mind opens to the possibilities of giving things away to your customers and potential customers, their minds will open to the possibility of becoming your customer for life.

14

One of the most valuable things that guerrilla companies give for free are free consultations. They are glorious door-openers. By offering them, you're giving your prospects an easy, no-risk way of seeing if you're as good as they want you to be. Have the insight to know *free consultations are ways to win customers with your expertise, not your salesmanship.*

When you offer free consultations, put a time limit on them. Make the offer of them simple to accept. A free consultation of no longer than one hour assures prospects that they won't be wasting a lot of time with you, and you'll be saving your own time as well.

During the consultation, ask questions, listen carefully to the answers, then do everything you can to help your prospects. Dig deeply to discover their problems, then try your darndest to solve them. Forget yourself for that hour and give yourself over as entirely as possible to the prospect. Don't worry about giving away the store. If it can be given away in an hour, it may not be of as much value as you think.

At the end of the hour, or fifteen minutes or whatever length you decide upon for your free consultations, you must offer to end the consultation. After all, you promised. If the prospect wants to continue talking, and you want to continue helping, that's all right. But still, you are obligated to bring the consultation to a close by the time you said it would close. Ideally, you'll learn how to prove your worth within that consultation time.

After the free consultation is over, you are entitled to make your bravest attempt to convert your prospect to a customer. If you did a good job during your free consultation, that shouldn't be very difficult. If you establish clear lines of communication, momentum is on your side.

What kinds of businesses should offer free consultations? A better question is, What kinds of businesses shouldn't? From hairdressers to attorneys, from manufacturers to retailers, from service businesses to service stations, almost every business can gain new customers by offering free consultations, for a free consultation is laden with value, the hope of new information, and freedom from risk for the prospect. The majority of people who will respond to it will be the most torrid of prospects.

You can offer your free consultations with advertising, direct mail, telemarketing, brochures, signs, online — in a variety of places. A free consultation is a high-powered, low-cost marketing weapon that you'll find you can use with increasing skill. Never underestimate the value of free personalized consulting.

15

Although a brochure alone is insufficient to fulfill your marketing plan, a brochure can bring you closer to your goal more cost-effectively than many other marketing weapons. *Brochures should be created for solid prospects and filled with the information they crave.*

With rare exceptions, guerrillas distribute their brochures only to people who request them. They make their brochures available in printed form, on videotape, or on audiotape. They may advertise their free brochures proudly in as many media as they can afford. Guerrillas give them to anyone who wants them, except to non-prospects, nonrequesters, or the general public.

One of the main purposes of a brochure is to furnish all the details about your business. The cost is horribly prohibitive to supply these details in the standard mass media — you'd need to buy a full-page newspaper ad, a two-page magazine ad, a ten-minute TV commercial, or a fifteen-minute radio spot.

Who cares about all the details? Prospects care. And they care like crazy. The last thing they want to do is make a mistake with a purchase. So they try to learn as much as they can before they part with their precious dollars. And until each and every one of your prospects is online and all guerrillas publish their brochures online, your prospects learn the details about your business from the brochures they request by phone or mail. The more details, the more features and benefits, the more testimonials and words of guarantee your brochure provides, the greater the chance your prospect will buy.

Guerrillas realize that if they put all the facts in a brochure designed for the general public, it would be boring to nonprospects regardless of its beauty. However, if they mail that same brochure to prospects only, it would be fascinating even if it were ugly.

When you produce a brochure, and it's easier than ever with the computer software that's available, keep these pointers in mind.

- **Try to make the sale at the end of your brochure.** Brochures should take prospects all the way to the ordering stage. Go for that order.
- **Make your brochure visually stimulating.** Use photos or illustrations, diagrams, or even cartoons to help prospects understand how they benefit.
- **You don't have to keep the copy short.** Supply a lot of information. If your copy is long, use subheads to break it up.
- **The entire message in your brochure should be timeless.** Write the copy as though it is three years from now. Will it still be accurate? Guerrillas love printing brochures, but not making revisions and reprinting those brochures.

16

Guerrillas learn how to gain the massive firepower that comes with being recognized as an expert. Guerrillas know that they should *freely offer their expertise to the public and be acknowledged as authorities in their field.*

How might you offer the wisdom that will earn credibility, customers, and profits for you? Today there are more ways than ever. Let's start with five.

1. *Write a column* for a local newspaper, industry magazine, or newsletter that reaches your prospects. Don't charge the publisher a cent. Just ask to be identified by your company name and phone number and Web site. See if they'll allow you to add a paragraph subtly tooting your own horn.
2. Haven't got time to write a regular column? Not a problem. *Write an article.* Again, don't charge for it, but do deflect all glory to your business and make it easy for readers to find you. When these columns and articles appear, make scads of reprints for future mailings and brochures.
3. *Offer your services as a speaker* to local clubs. They are always alert for lunchtime speakers to come in to talk for half an hour or so. If you can speak without selling and can impart

worthwhile information, you'll see how this untapped venue for guerrillas is a royal road to bigtime credibility.

4. *Publish a column online.* If you think local clubs are hungry for speakers, wait till you see how starved the Internet is for good content. If you can supply it, in the form of a daily, weekly, or monthly online column in an Internet section readily accessed by your prospects, you're in guerrilla clover. Publish your column through a big online service, in a newsgroup, or on one of the many Web sites happy to have you.

5. *Host an online conference.* If you have truly helpful information, ask one of the online services if you can host a conference. Don't forget — at the conference you shouldn't make a sales presentation. But you have a golden opportunity to prove your expertise and begin lasting relationships.

You can save and print a transcript of your conference for use in other marketing materials. Even if you host it in 2000, it can give you credibility in 2010. Timeliness and timelessness are characteristics of the guerrilla.

These methods enable you to become an authority to many people at the same time. They do not ask you to invest one cent of your money, but in true guerrilla fashion, require that you be willing to devote time, energy, and imagination. There are many other methods, such as publishing a newsletter, hosting a segment on TV, having a radio show, or appearing as a guest expert, for you to carry your guerrilla banner forward into the fray without writing checks for the privilege. All guerrilla arsenals are well stocked with plans to gain credibility and the beautiful bottom line that goes along with it.

17

One of the most overlooked marketing weapons is customer referrals. The cost of an active referral program is tiny compared with the potential for profits such a program can mean. *Guerrillas have the insight to know their greatest source of new customers is old customers.* The best way to get the names of new customers from old customers? *Simply ask for them.*

As a guerrilla, you've been staying in touch, so your customers want you to succeed and will happily comply with your request for, say, three names. Ask for them, provide a postage-paid envelope, and you'll soon see this tactic is pure gold. There are other ways to tap into your enormous referral power.

- **Identify potential references.** List everyone with whom you have worked in the past three years, and others who know you well.
- **Note on your list what you would like a reference to do.** There is more than one kind of reference: use of their name, calls made for you, and written testimonials. Be specific. Think especially of what you would like past customers to say. You'll be surprised at how willing they are to say it.
- **Ask pleasantly.** Asking politely generates good references. Everybody understands the need for a business reference. It's a

reasonable thing to ask for. If properly asked, most people will applaud good work.

- **Request name use.** First, phone and ask the potential references if you can use their names — either in talking with a potential customer or on your company brochure. Allow them the chance to say no.
- **Get telephone references.** You can tell by people's voice tones if their references will be good. If references agree to your using their names, ask if they will take phone inquiries. Create a stable of references who will speak highly of you when called.
- **Obtain a letter.** If the telephone reference is better than average, ask for it in writing. Tell the reference that a few short words will do, such as, "Ms. Atwood's service was outstanding. We intend to use her on 90 percent of our future jobs."

Why don't people give more referrals? Because they're afraid you'll foul up and they'll be blamed. Guerrillas continue to *develop new customers all the time* because they know they're losing old customers all the time for the following reasons:

1 percent of customers die
3 percent move away
5 percent develop other business relationships
9 percent leave for competitive reasons
14 percent are dissatisfied with the product or service
68 percent leave due to an indifference on the part
of an employee

The way around these irrevocable statistics? With a referral program that is active, alive, constantly used, and part of the way you run your business.

18

I f you've been keeping up on things guerrilla, you can't help but notice how many businesses have banded together for marketing projects. They go in jointly on the costs of special events, TV commercials, print ads, and direct marketing, in a blazing spirit of cooperation and mutual helpfulness. The name for this never-to-die phenomenon is fusion marketing. And in an era of fierce competition, savvy business owners know that they must *fuse it or lose it.*

Fusion marketing enables you to extend your marketing reach and pep up your marketing frequency. It's easy to afford because you're sharing the cost with others. They're putting up signs for you as you're putting up signs for them. They're mentioning your firm in their consultations, making it easy for you to mention theirs. They put your name in their brochure. You put their name in yours. Everybody gains, especially the customers who have learned to trust you.

The idea is to stop thinking about competition for a while and to focus on cooperation. Think of the businesses with which you can connect so that both of you benefit. The obvious choice for businesses to link with are those that have the same kind of prospects that you do. In fact, some businesses form what they call "leads clubs." In these clubs, businesses with the same kind of prospects share leads at the end of each month. Marketing costs tumble as a result, and profits rise.

Look for companies that could benefit by filling in gaps in their service with the offerings of yours. Restaurants that don't deliver fuse naturally with delivery services. Gas stations that don't offer car washes fuse like brothers with nearby car washes. Video recorder stores fuse with videotape stores. Photography stores fuse with framing stores. CPAs fuse with lawyers, creative consultants with media consultants. Do I make my point?

You'll find fusion partners online everywhere. And you'll notice that the smartest ones have links all over the Internet. They link to Web sites that offer links back to them. The fusion marketing partners gain. The Internet surfers gain. And business, needing less money to market, turns its attention to quality and service, so the world gains.

This mutual aid society is also known as co-marketing, tie-ins with others, collaborative marketing, and lots of other fancy appellations. But the concept probably dates back as far as the caveman who hawked his animal skins from cave to cave. The guy in the next cave probably said, "Grunt good things about my nuts and berries when you make your cave calls. When I make mine, I'll grunt good things about your furs."

19

Advertising is the most visible of all forms of marketing and it's the one that most business owners misunderstand the most. When they begin advertising, they think they are now marketing. But the truth is that when they begin advertising, they are now advertising. There are one hundred weapons of marketing, and advertising is only one of them. It may be the most expensive and the most abused, too.

Guerrillas know that *advertising is the icing and the other weapons of marketing are the cake.* You can't satisfy most of your prospects with icing only. As delicious it is, it's not much without the cake.

You must have many other parts of the marketing process baked and ready to serve before you layer on the icing. Be sure your salespeople are trained, your phones are answered properly, you have a referral system up and running, your signs are clear, your selection is up to snuff, your employees know how to upgrade the size of sale. Such details must be attended to before the advertising runs.

When it does run, the salespeople will function better because they'll have real prospects to talk to. It will make your direct mail more successful; your telemarketing will come to life because people will have heard of you. It will turn your referral program from a good idea into a profit-producing machine. It will let you sell items you didn't even advertise, items that prospects learned of when they visited or contacted you.

On its own, advertising is usually somewhat ineffective. Added to your arsenal, however, advertising takes on a whole new meaning and becomes lethal in the hands of a prepared guerrilla. It enhances every other marketing weapon. The biggest problem involving advertising is not the advertising itself, but those advertisers who are clueless as to what advertising can and cannot do. Twice in my life I have bought something strictly because of the advertising and the moment after I had been exposed to the advertising. In every other instance it has taken a long time for the advertising to take effect.

The same is true for your prospects. Generally, they don't buy products or services immediately as a result of advertising. They buy these things eventually. Most advertisers do not understand this and suspect that their advertising has been poorly conceived or placed in the wrong media unless it delivers instant results. They pull their ads and waste their investment, believing that advertising doesn't work for them. Advertising changes people's attitudes *over time.* It cannot work miracles instantly. Whew! I'm glad you're clear on that now. I detest the thought of any guerrilla wasting one penny.

20

How can you tell a guerrilla from a non-guerrilla? The non-guerrilla thinks that marketing is over the moment a sale has been consummated. But the guerrilla understands that the marketing *begins* once the sale has been made. The guerrilla may not have made a whole lot of money on that single transaction, but will earn a whale of a lot over a long timespan — strictly because *the guerrilla is always aware of the extraordinary power of follow-up.* What is the guerrilla's middle name? Follow-up.

Exactly what does follow-up mean to a guerrilla? It means listening to what the prospect says after the sale is over. It means giving the customer something over and above the transaction value, such as a free gift relating to the purchase, a guarantee, a piece of valuable advice, inside information, something the customer didn't buy and didn't expect. Call it an overvalue if you will. Buy a bed from my friend Michael and he'll toss in a free set of sheets and pillowcases after the sale has been closed. Is this why his business becomes more profitable every year? Take a guess.

To a guerrilla, follow-up means staying in touch. This is crucial. Nearly 70 percent of business is lost not because of poor quality or shabby service, but because of customers being ignored after the sale. Guerrillas stay in touch and do it with care and warmth by employing a variety of follow-up tools, all based on information about the customer. Follow-up weapons, in the hands of a guerrilla, are thank-you notes after the sale, phone calls inquiring as to whether the customer has any questions, a direct-mail letter calling attention to a new item related to the item purchased by the customer, newsletters, frequent buyer club invitations, advance notice of new offerings or special sales, birthday cards on the customer's birthday, anniversary cards on the anniversary of the customer becoming a customer, research questionnaires, and letters asking for the names of people who should get on the mailing list. The list goes on and on, as should the follow-up.

Customers show their gratitude with repeat purchases, with abundant referrals, with a long-standing relationship with your business, even with recommending potential fusion partners. Guerrilla follow-up makes your business a part of your customer's identity. It separates you from most of the other businesses in town — indeed, on the whole planet.

Do you know why the ideas of staying in touch, proving that you care, and intensifying your customer relationships with contact are called follow-up? Because when you've won their hearts, their money and their business, their referrals and their loyalty will follow, and your profits will increase.

CHAPTER FOUR

INSIGHTS INTO
MEDIA

21

All the media available to you have specific strengths and weaknesses, so the way you state your message or offer usually must differ from medium to medium. If you don't capitalize on the power of the medium in which you're marketing, you may be wasting your money. Few things are changing faster than the media, and guerrillas know that if they're not keeping up to date, they're falling behind.

What's happening is that the media are becoming far more accessible to small businesses. Tiny companies that couldn't dream of affording a TV campaign are discovering that cable TV makes the tube very affordable. Those who thought that advertising in a major magazine was a fantasy are delighted to learn of the low cost of regional editions of that magazine. Costs are dropping and the media are getting hungrier because of inroads made by the newest medium of all — the Internet. The prime benefactors? Small businesses. Especially the guerrillas in their midst.

Where companies rarely thought twice about classified advertising, now they see it as an economical way to reach carefully targeted prospects. One reason the Internet is so valuable to guerrillas is simply because of the enormous number of classified ads — many of them absolutely free to place. And each year, new classifications appear in the classified section of newspapers. "Internet

Consultants," "Telephone Equipment," "Personal Computers," "Bankruptcy Assistance," and "Employment Alternatives" are just a few of the many new classifications for reaching limitless prospects with a limited budget. Online, there are hundreds more. *The Internet offers guerrillas more opportunities than ever.*

Many magazines that once disdained classified ads now feature classified sections — in the back of the magazine. Research indicates that 61 percent of Americans read magazines from back to front, an inordinately high readership for a relatively tiny investment. Guerrillas can tantalize readers with crucial data *and* an enticing offer of a free brochure.

Guerrillas, knowing the brute force of a headline, treat their classified messages as *all headline,* presenting their offers cogently and clearly. Some use the classified ads as the first step of a continuing process; others attempt to close the sale with the ad. Both tactics work if they're approached with the understanding that classified ads are read by the hottest of the hot prospects. A guerrilla's arsenal brims with weapons large and small. Classified ads are small but can make a large impact on profits. Today, they're worth your consideration more than ever before.

22

Television is still the king of the marketing hill, enabling you to reach right- and left-brained people, to present your story visually and verbally, to add the emotional ambiance of music, to demonstrate, to show before-and-after graphic presentations, and to home in to your exact target audience. TV was once available only to those with deep pockets, but today it is also available to those with insight.

The cost of a prime-time commercial slot on cable TV in any major market in America is less than $20. This means that guerrillas can advertise on any cable-delivered station. ESPN, CNN, the Discovery Channel, Arts and Entertainment, MTV — all of those and more are within the reach of guerrillas.

Better still, cable TV allows guerrillas to accurately target the neighborhoods they wish to reach. Instead of blanketing a city with commercials and reaching people who are too far to do business with them, guerrillas can direct their spots only to the communities in which their prospects live. One guerrilla I know directs his only to the most affluent zip codes in a large metropolitan area. Another aims his only to people who stay up late.

Satellite TV, growing very rapidly, represents still another fertile ground for guerrillas. The cost of running national spots beamed from satellites is often less than $100 for a 30-second message.

Television is a *visual* medium — 70 percent of viewers mute commercials. And so guerrillas tell their story *visually.* Don't depend on the sound. Rather than hiring expensive talent, rely on the stunning force of a brilliant idea.

The average cost to produce a 30-second TV commercial ran close to $200,000 in 1998 — usually for beer, fast-food chains, athletic shoe, and soft drink advertisements. However, a commercial can cost less than $1,000 if the idea is powerful and the advertiser relies upon it rather than on fancy special effects. Cable companies are specializing in teaching guerrillas how to decrease production costs while increasing the response to a spot. Guerrillas use tight scripts and serious rehearsals; guerrillas produce the soundtrack first, then shoot silent footage to go with it; and they produce several commercials at the same time. And I'm not talking about cheap-looking spots; I'm referring to expensive-looking spots without the expense. The pot is larger than ever and the ante is smaller.

23

R adio didn't disappear with the advent of TV, just as movies didn't drop off the face of the earth. *Radio is bigger and better than ever, more effective than ever, too.* Guerrillas in record numbers are using it, even for direct marketing, making an offer and requiring a toll-free call for the buyer to accept it.

Guerrillas can target their audiences with pinpoint accuracy using radio. Whether their audience is teenagers, Hispanics, sports buffs, newshounds, motorists, or women aged 34 to 45, there's a radio station beaming right to those people. In many cases, these people have made the radio station a part of their identity and so they believe what the station announcers say.

Guerrillas make certain those announcers have tried the products about to be advertised so as to obtain the benefit of both an announcement and an endorsement. Often, the 30 seconds they pay for blossoms into three minutes because the announcer waxes enthusiastically about his or her wonderful experience with the product or service. If you thought you can't buy credibility like that, guerrillas have learned that you can indeed.

Each radio advertising guerrilla divides radio stations into two prime categories — foreground radio, which requires active listening, and is typified by news shows, sports shows, talk shows and religious shows — and background radio, which requires only passive listening, and is typified by musical programming, anywhere from top forty to classical.

Repetition is paramount in making any radio commercial effective: repetition of the company name, repetition of the prime benefit or offer, repetition of the commercial. It must be aired several times a day, several days a week, at least three weeks out of four, and consistently through the year or at least the primary selling season.

Some people think humor is just the ticket for radio but I think humor is just the ticket for oblivion if you're going to also rely on repetition. Few things are more grating than a joke that is repeated endlessly. Jingles work very well on radio, especially if they're in the musical genre of the station. I was involved with the first rock-and-roll commercials to air on rock-and-roll radio, and I know sales rock and rolled for the duration of the campaign. Today, rock-and-roll commercials are standard fare on stations that play that kind of music.

The cost of radio is exceedingly low when you consider how many members of your target audience that you can reach over and over again; no other medium allows for such one-to-one intimacy.

24

To supplement the media you are using, for example, the radio, television, and a Web site — if your product or service is sold on the retail level — you should also state your message on a sign.

A full 74 percent of all purchase decisions in 1998 were made right at the time and place of purchase. People walk into a store with a vague notion of making a purchase, but those notions aren't solidified until the person is ready to buy. And what do you suppose solidifies the notions?

Signs do. *Signs connect your other marketing to the purchase experience.* They carry the selling momentum from the marketing arenas into the store itself. They allow retailers to merchandise the things people came in to buy and cross-merchandise those items people didn't even realized that you offered. Signs generate impulse purchases.

Your signs should tie in clearly with your marketing strategy — your identity, your niche, your theme. Your signs must have the same colors, type styles, and design elements that are present in your other marketing; this helps your prospective customers make the connection.

Signs are not only used by guerrillas in stores, they're also used throughout the community on bulletin boards. Most communities in the world have community bulletin boards where people post fliers, notices, three-by-five cards listing things for sale or rent, almost anything. In the San Francisco Bay area, where I live, more than eight hundred such locations have been identified, and several companies have sprung up to service these locations for guerrillas who want to reach their target markets regularly at less than $100 a month.

As with classified ads, signs should be thought of as all head-line. Some sign experts peg six as the maximum number of words that should appear on a sign. But that's primarily a billboard ad-age, and you have my permission to use as many words as you'd like on your community bulletin board sign.

The creative placement of signs is also a guerrilla trait. Some businesses place their signs only one block from their competitors' establishments. Others think of creative places for signs, such as airports, taxis, restaurants, buses, and sports arenas. A sign can rarely serve as your whole selling job — unless it is at the place of purchase. But signs can remind, bring on impulse reactions, and pay off your expensive marketing without much expense.

Guerrilla retailers tell me that the very best of all signs is a red neon sign than says "open." Makes sense to me.

25

I t also makes sense to me that telemarketing is growing so rapidly. Telemarketing is used more often than direct mail and has been since 1982. It works better in business-to-business relationships but is also used by companies calling individuals — especially during dinnertime, I've noticed.

Telemarketing works best if it connects with other marketing you've done, if it is part of a campaign that also includes direct mail, and if it is accomplished by scripts instead of thought-flow outlines. In any sales organization, 20 percent of the personnel making calls accomplish 80 percent of the sales. This is no accident — those 20 percent, the most successful telemarketers, use magic words and phrases and stress certain ideas and benefits.

If scripts are prepared that contain those words and phrases, those ideas and benefits — and if they are memorized so that they sound as though they're spoken direct from the heart — everybody's sales are going to rise. Your next job is to get them to rise even higher by improving the quality of the words, phrases, ideas, and benefits.

Insight into the primary benefits of telemarketing teaches you that they allow you not only to establish rapport with the person you're calling, but also to actually make an offer and close the sale. Talk about interactive!

The key part of the call is the first five seconds. That's when you're either going to gain or lose the attention of the caller, turn that person into a friend or a foe. A few ways to get the relationship warmed up:

- Give your name to the person you're calling.
- Tell the person why you're calling.
- Speak very clearly and with a smile in your voice.
- Say something lighthearted, even humorous.
- Ask a question to which the answer is yes.
- Tell how long the phone call will take; the shorter the better.

It takes skin the thickness of the polar ice cap to be a successful telemarketer. The rejection rate is so high that professional callers are delighted just to get to the people they're calling rather than being deterred by gatekeepers. Guerrillas get close to gatekeepers by learning their names and treating them honestly and with civility, allowing the gates to be opened.

If for every six phone calls you get through only once and if for every time you get through you close only one in ten sales, start thinking in terms of sixty. For every sixty calls you make, you make one sale. How many groups of sixty can you reach in one day? If you build rejection into your plan, you will travel far beyond rejection and toward profitability.

26

A key fact is that *all the media work better if they're supported by the other media.* Advertise your Web site on your TV commercial. Mention your advertising in your direct mail. Refer to your direct mail in your telemarketing. Plant the seeds of your offering with some kinds of marketing and fertilize them with other kinds.

You're not really promoting unless you're cross-promoting. Your trade show booth will be far more valuable to you if you promote it in trade magazines and with fliers put under the doors of hotels near the trade show. Guerrillas try to market their marketing.

Your prospects, being humans, are eclectic people. They pay attention to a lot of media. Therefore, you can't depend on a mere one medium to motivate a purchase. You must introduce a notion, remind people of it, say it again, and then repeat it using different words somewhere else. Successful guerrillas combine several media. They say in their ads, "Call or write for our free brochure." They say in their Yellow Pages ad, "Get even more details at our Web site." They enclose a copy of their magazine ad in their mailings. They enlarge the magazine ad to use as a sign. Their Web site features their print ads.

Guerrillas are quick to mention their use of one medium while using another. People equate a broad-scale marketing campaign with quality and success; they trust names they've heard of over strange and new names. People also ignore most marketing messages — often intentionally. The remote control is not only a way to avoid getting off the couch but also a method of avoiding marketing messages.

No matter how glorious your newspaper campaign may be, your prospects don't all read the paper, so you need to grab them in another way. And no matter how dazzling your Web site, it's like a grain of sand in a desert if it is not pointed out to an unknowing and basically uncaring public.

Cross-promoting in the media is another way to accomplish the all-important task of repetition. One way to implant your message is to *repeat it*. Another is to say it in several different places. Guerrillas try to do both. Nothing is left to chance. If you saw a Yellow Pages ad that made you an offer from a company you'd never heard of and another with the same offer but that also mentioned, "As advertised on television," you'd probably opt for the second because of that added smidgen of credibility. I rest my case.

27

The Yellow Pages, adorned with red, blue, white, and green printing, not to mention photographs in black and white or full-color, represent a torrid opportunity to guerrillas. *Nobody reads the Yellow Pages for entertainment value or dazzling beauty.* Everybody consulting the directory is looking for information or to look up a phone number. In many cases these people, potential lifelong customers, are perched at the threshold of a buying decision.

Guerrillas are quick to move these people from the ranks of prospects to the ranks of customers. They do this in several intriguing ways, and in some cases, with a combination of intriguing methods. Let's examine four tips for advertising in the Yellow Pages so that the people who are letting their fingers do the walking become the people who do the purchasing from you.

a. Guerrillas use a color to flag the attention of browsers. Which color? Whichever their competitors aren't using. If all their competitors are using a color they stand out by not using one. They use their colors in their border, headline, background or all of these.

b. Guerrillas purchase the largest ad in the Yellow Pages section, which assures that they'll be up front when people go through the section — ideally reading from front to back, though we both know it doesn't always work that way. Large-sized Yellow Page ads cost large amounts of money and generate large numbers of responses. What's best? Measure for yourself.

c. Guerrillas list all the services and benefits they offer. Since those who consult the directory are looking for information, the more information you can give them, the better. Pretty is good, but loaded with data is more than good. Don't forget, people are hankering for information and not for art.

d. Guerrillas look upon crowded sections as blessings in disguise. If you offer gardening services and there are four pages that list gardening services, your ad might state, "Free Telephone Consulting on How to Select a Gardener." Browsers tempted by such an offer often take advantage of the free consulting and end up as customers of the consultant.

Don't think that it is absolutely necessary that you advertise in the Yellow Pages — because it isn't. Only if people expect to find businesses like yours in the directory should you list your business there. Which phone directory to use? The biggest and most popular. A word to the wise: never tell anyone you're in the Yellow Pages, because you'll be directing them to your competitors. Be there if you want to be, but keep it to yourself.

28

*I*t is possible to use the media for no cost. There are several ways to accomplish this: barter, public relations, co-op, funds, and fusion marketing.

During the 1990s, more than half the mass media purchased was not purchased at all, but bartered for. The media are selling smoke. If they don't sell their smoke by a specific date, it disappears. Their radio and TV time, if unsold — it's up in smoke. Their magazine and newspaper space, if unsold — it's up in smoke. So the people selling time and space will bargain as they get close to their closing dates, and many will barter.

Perhaps you're offering a product or a service that they can use. Possibly one of their clients can use it. If not, possibly they'll contact a barter house. Maybe that's a good thing for you as well. To get an idea of how to do it, call 714-831-0607 for a free brochure. Steven Spielberg's isn't the only Lost World. Wait till you discover the world of barter.

Look also into gaining free media coverage through the art of public relations. The two disadvantages to PR are that you have little control over when it happens and what the media say about you, and if you do love what they said, it's very difficult to get repeat coverage. It's not like an ad that you can run again and again. Instead, it's news that runs only once.

The fact that it's news is one of its biggest advantages, along with being free. That means that if you can come up with something newsy about your product or service, there's a good chance you'll receive free media coverage. If your story is visually exciting, you might get free TV publicity. A small printing business developed a machine that made an enormous sign. They paraded the sign down the main street and the local TV station picked up the news. If your story has depth and fascination, offer yourself as a guest on a radio talk show or for an exclusive interview with a magazine. *The more media contacts you have, the more free media coverage you'll receive.*

Guerrillas who sell nationally advertised products can frequently get co-op funds, a fancy phrase meaning money, for mentioning the name of the national advertiser in their own advertising. I've met several who were able to name-drop so adroitly that the co-op funds covered the cost of the media — making them free to the guerrilla.

The same is true for guerrillas who engage in fusion marketing arrangements, for example, an offer to put up a sign for one marketing partner in return for a mention in their newspaper ad. Free media for both guerrillas. Good deal for both as well. Very guerrilla-like.

29

Guerrillas use magazines differently than other business owners use them. *No other medium offers as much pure credibility as magazines.* Guerrillas use business magazines in the normal manner — constant presence, cohesive identity, consistent visual format — going for the sale or the relationship with each advertisement.

In consumer magazines, go strictly for the credibility or the relationship and not for the sale. Because guerrillas cannot run a magazine schedule that will make an adequate impact on their audience, there are three tricks that make magazines end up paying off so well that they act like goldmines made of paper.

1. Scout out regional editions of national magazines. Call 800-225-3457 for a free brochure. That $90,000 for a full-page black-and-white ad in the national edition of a magazine runs only $1,500 in a local edition — right in the community where your prospects live.
2. Run your ads in one regional edition one time only — you'll go to the bank because of the reprints. Create timeless ads that do not say silly things like "Our company is five years old" because next year, when the firm is six, the ad will be dated. Instead, state "We were founded in 1995," because your ad

won't date itself. Do not print pictures of employees, for one might end up a serial killer. Who knows? Can't be too careful if you're a guerrilla.

3. Order zillions of reprints of your ad, each emblazoned with the credibility-building "As advertised in *Time* magazine" (or other publication). Reprints are available, at costs that delight guerrillas, as regular reprints, as laminated reprints, as one-page self-mailers, as four-page self-mailers, as easel-back window signs, as self-standing A-frame signs, and in many other guises. Guerrillas then post the reprints all over creation and do mailings in which they enclose one. Some guerrillas in the late 1990s are still sending mailings in which they enclose a reprint of an ad they ran in the early 1970s.

Today, magazine advertising may be the wisest and most profitable investment you'll make. The key is to *not* expect from the media only what convention has led you to expect. The media delivers best when you have insight into their affordability. You are known by the company you keep, and magazines keep you amidst the very best company.

30

S ome media fall into the apple category; other media into the orange category, and what works in one medium may not work in another. *Guerrillas have insight into the powers of each medium* and use each to its greatest advantages. This is what you should know about media power.

- **The power of newspapers is news.** If you are advertising in a newspaper, a newsy ad will get noticed because news is in the forefront of readers' minds.
- **The power of magazines is credibility.** Readers unconsciously attach to the advertiser the same credibility that they associate with the magazine.
- **The power of radio is intimacy.** Radio is typically a one-on-one situation that allows for an intimate connection between listener and marketer.
- **The power of direct mail is urgency.** Dated offers that will expire often motivate prospects to act now.
- **The power of telemarketing is rapport.** Few media allow you to establish two-way rapport as adroitly as the phone.
- **The power of a brochure is the ability to give details.** Few media allow you the time and space to expand on your benefits as much as a brochure.

- **The power of classified ads is information.** Nobody in their right mind actually reads the classified ads except those in a quest for data.
- **The power of the Yellow Pages is detailed information.** Here prospects will compare the information that's provided.
- **The power of television is the ability to demonstrate.** No other medium lets you show your product or service in use along with the benefits it offers. TV is still the undisputed heavyweight champ of marketing.
- **The power of the Internet is interactivity.** On the Internet you can flag people's attention, inform them, answer their questions, and take their orders.
- **The power of signs is impulse reactions.** Signs motivate people to buy if they are in a buying mood and in a buying arena. Signs can trigger consumers' impulses and remind them of your other marketing or both.
- **The power of fliers is economy.** Fliers can be created, produced, and distributed for very little money, and they can deliver instant results.
- **The power of billboards is to remind.** Billboards rarely do the whole selling job, but they jostle people's thoughts about your other marketing efforts.

Guerrillas are aware of the specific powers of each medium and design their marketing so as to capitalize upon them. Their awareness gives them more mileage for their marketing investments than if they created marketing while being oblivious to these special strengths. By capitalizing on their insights, they get the very most that each of the media have to offer. Adjusting the message to the medium is an artform and a necessity.

All media were not created equal. Guerrillas are quick to take advantage of these inequalities to increase the effectiveness of each weapon they use.

CHAPTER FIVE

INSIGHTS INTO ONLINE MARKETING

31

The newest, biggest, most mysterious, most misunderstood, and most promising marketing opportunity in history is the one offered by the advent of the Internet. Every day, online marketing gets bigger, better, and more helpful both for marketers and for consumers. Still, three facts must be understood by all who would hope to become online guerrillas:

a. Online marketing will only work if you understand marketing.
b. Online marketing means a lot more than having a Web site.
c. Online marketing is only 1 percent of all marketing.

Remember that there are at least one hundred marketing weapons and that online marketing is only one of them. In most cases, you can't market online only with any expectation of success. Yet, the entire media world is becoming fragmented. There are regional editions of magazines, zone editions of newspapers, cable TV stations that reach local communities, local radio stations, targeted mailing lists. Where does everything come together?

It all happens online. Slowly but certainly, people are learning that the whole story exists online — that all the details they must learn before making a purchase are ready to be studied online. The entire Internet phenomenon is part of human evolution, and humans learning how to interact in cyberspace is also part of evolution. You don't have to be reminded that evolution takes place over a long period of time. The Internet is here and everybody knows it, but not everybody is online yet, and not everybody online is ready to make purchases yet. They will be. But not quite yet.

The insight is that *you must continue marketing with traditional media.* Your Web site needs marketing. Even when the Internet has achieved a market penetration comparable to that of the telephone, you must continue marketing using time-honored methods. TV revolutionized the marketing scene, but most of the big TV advertisers also market their offerings in places other than the tube. TV is part of their marketing mix, but not the entire potion.

When marketing with the traditional media, you're going to have to devote time and space to heralding your Web site because many people will want to know where they can get more information. Your Web site is where. No media offers you the comprehensiveness of the Web. That's why you need it to flesh out your marketing. The world is learning to buy things in a new way and that way is online. But the learning process is still in process.

32

Pinning down the right way to do guerrilla marketing online is akin to grabbing a handful of smoke to see what it feels like. Online marketing is the essence of amorphousness and will be for a long time, constantly changing as new heroes of technology try to figure how it can best serve the public while bestowing profits upon the companies employing it. Exciting online technologies are being unveiled so frequently they're becoming humdrum.

Of the billions of dollars being wasted by small businesses due to a misunderstanding of the comprehensiveness of online marketing and the reality of online consumers, a huge portion is wasted on Web sites. They are created and posted with obliviousness to their place in the cosmos. Guerrillas wouldn't dare waste money on their Web sites. They know the ground rules in cyberspace when it comes to earning consistent profits on the Web. Those profits come when you *equally emphasize eight elements.*

The first element is planning. That means you must know ahead of time exactly what you wish to accomplish with your Web site.
The second element is content. That's what's going to attract visitors to your site, then keep them coming back for more visits on a regular basis.

The third element is design. There's a "hang or click" moment when people first see your site. Should they hang around or click away? Design influences their decision.

The fourth element is involvement. Guerrillas take advantage of the net's interactivity by involving visitors rather than just requiring that they read.

The fifth element is production. This refers to putting your first four elements online. Easy-to-use software now can do this job for you.

The sixth element is follow-up. People visit your site, e-mail you, ask or answer some questions. Guerrillas respond to their e-mail, stay in touch.

The seventh element is promotion. You must promote your site online by registering with search engines and linking with other sites, while promoting it offline in mass media, mailings, wherever your name appears.

The eighth element is maintenance. Unlike other marketing, a Web site requires constant changing, updating, freshening, renewing. Like a baby.

It was once believed that Web sites had to be long to be valuable, but the increased awareness of the precious nature of time is causing online marketers to rethink this concept. Web sites narrowly targeted to specific groups are brief and valuable. Guerrillas know the value of being concise. An overall Web site may be vast, but within it are tiny segments targeted with precision for small niches. In this way, huge guerrilla companies can have the warmth and close connection of small guerrilla start-ups.

33

O nce you've got even the spark of a notion to go online, let that spark ignite thoughts of how you'll promote your site. Have the insight to know *this means thinking imaginatively about two worlds.*

The first is the online world, where you'll think in terms of multiple links to other sites, banners leading to your site, search engines directing browsers to your site, postings on forums alerting onliners to your site, chat conferences heralding your site, recommendations of your site by Internet powers, e-mailing to parties demonstrably interested in learning about the topics covered on your site, writing articles for other sites in return for links back to your site, mentioning your site in your e-mail signature, advertising online to entice people to your site, preparing an online version of your press kit to publicize your site online, and connecting with as many other online entities as possible, all in a quest to make your site part of the online community, an Internet landmark to your prospects, a not-be-missed feature of the Web.

The second world in which your imagination should run rampant in a mission to achieve top-of-the-mind awareness of your site is the offline world. Most of the population of the real world still resides there. That's where they continue to get most of their information — for now. And that's where you've got to let them know of your online site — teeming with information that can shower them with benefits — for their business or their lives or both.

Tout your site in your ads, on stationery, on your business cards, on signs, on brochures, fliers, Yellow Pages ads, advertising specialties, packages, business forms, gift certificates, reprints of PR articles, in your catalog, newsletter, and classified ads. Mention it in your radio spots, on television. More than one company now has a jingle heralding their Web site. Never neglect to direct folks to your site in direct-mail letters and postcards, in all your faxes, almost anywhere your name appears. If the world begins to think that your last name is dotcom, you're going about your offline promotional activities in the right way.

Some companies think that by mentioning their site in tiny letters at the bottom of their ad or by flashing it at the end of their TV commercial, they're taking care of their offline promotion. But they're not — they're only going through the motions. Talk about your Web site the same way you would about your child — with pride, enthusiasm, and joy. Make people excited about your site! Let them see your pride! Will local or industry newspapers write about your online site? Of course they will, if you make it fascinating enough for their readers. That's *your* job. Promotion will lure them to your site, killer content will cause them to make return trips.

34

Of the multitude of errors made while attempting to market online, the biggest is treating your online efforts the same as you treat your offline efforts. It's a different ballgame that is being played in cyberspace, and although the basic rules of marketing continue to apply, there are new rules to follow as well. The first rule is to *pay close attention*.

To what should you be paying attention? Begin with your own Web site, making certain that it is continually fresh and enticing. Pay extra close attention to how easy it is to find you. Does your site appear near the top in all the search engines? Is it on the first page of any classified search? Can visitors directly access the data they need rather than having to navigate through many unnecessary pages? Is it simple to contact you? Do all the links you provide continue to link to onliners with whom you wish to continue collaborating? What are your competitors saying? Which newsgroups are centered around your business or industry? What new changes are coming about that might add spark and pep to your online marketing campaign?

When you create a TV spot, you send it to the TV station and watch it run. There's little else to do. But when you create a Web site, that's just the start. Do you retrieve your e-mail at least twice a day? If not, e-mailers might think you're lax on the job. I've often sent e-mail to businesses, only to phone them a few days later due to a lack of response and hear them say, "Oh, we better check our e-mail more often. We didn't get around to it yet this week."

The guerrilla's single greatest online error is to overly rely on his or her Web site. Merely having a site doesn't mean you're an active online marketer. To be active in cyberspace, you must be *active* in the many forums in which your prospects participate. Read what they say. Participate. Post messages that prove your expertise. Send e-mail to members of the forum because they have already demonstrated interest in the topic.

The same is true for chat rooms. Many are devoted to the same subject to which your business is devoted. Become active in those chat rooms; they are superb opportunities to establish close, one-to-one, lasting relationships. You must never be crass in those rooms, blaring out your business pitch, but if you're sensitive to the tenor of the conversation and you're paying close attention, you can accomplish quite a bit. And for zero money.

Being active in forums and chat groups, e-mailing actively but only to those who want your e-mail, keeping abreast of online search technology, *and* having a regularly maintained and vigorously promoted Web site — that's how to do it. Doing any less is a major error on your part.

35

Once you are online, you must knock yourself out *maintaining maximum visibility* for your site. One way to do this is with aggressive offline promoting. Another is with a relentless e-mail campaign. A third is to continually post messages in special interest groups. A fourth is to establish a plethora of links to sites that wish to attract the same kind of prospects as you.

It is crucial that you know your way around the ever-changing search engines so you can keep your site visible to all who might be a prospect. Equally important is to repackage your content and present it anew. Cereals and laundry detergents haven't changed much over the years, but if you were to study the boxes as they appear on supermarket shelves, you'd think everything about them is new. It isn't. It's just served up a new way.

Guerrillas revere the idea of repetition. However, repetition is more applicable to the real world than to cyberspace. In its fast-paced environment, information grows stale very fast. An ad that reappears in a newspaper projects a consistent and stable image. But if you rerun the same content on a Web site, prospects think you're asleep at the mouse. They're not even certain you're still in business.

To remain visible, repackage your messages to the same audience. Repackage your products and expose them to new markets. Be on a continuing quest to find new locations so you can expand your market.

You can add to your visibility by hosting online conferences, publishing tip sheets or online newsletters, and by being written up in offline publications read by onliners. Such publications include *Home Office Computing, Internet World, NetGuide,* and a galaxy of others.

Your online marketing plan will be successful if you understand what your prospects really want: safety, convenience, speed, service, information, personal attention, and good values. Offer them what they're looking for and orient your online marketing to those needs.

Increase your visibility by listing your site in every directory that your prospects might check. Consider national directories, but don't overlook local or regional directories. Establish links on as many of those directory pages as possible. There are one hundred different guerrilla marketing online weapons, all listed in Chapter 10 of *Guerrilla Marketing Online.* Each one will increase your visibility even more. The insight I impart to you here is that *in cyberspace, you're invisible* — unless you do something about it — and continue doing something to make yourself impossible to miss.

36

The content of your Web site should include the information *your prospects and customers want to know the most*. It's not necessarily the content you want to put forth and boast about. Instead, it's data about how your company can have a positive impact on visitors to your site.

To create the best content, work backward, beginning with the goals you wish to reach with your site. Put into writing *the specific goals* you wish your Web site to achieve for you. The more specific you are, the more likely you are to hit those goals.

Next, put into writing the obstacles that may stand in the way of your company attaining its goals. Such obstacles are typically a lack of information by your target audience. Therefore, you need to become a bridge-builder. Build a bridge between your goals and your target audience. Construct it of valuable information.

Your Web site will succeed or fail based on how much overlap there is between its content and the needs of your target audiences. Exquisite design and spectacular promotion are meaningless if their content doesn't fill the needs of the market. It's not that difficult to develop that kind of content. Following is a list of seventeen important questions. Answer these questions, for your specific answers will provide your content:

- What is the immediate, short-term goal of your Web site?
- What specific action do you want visitors to take?
- What are your specific objectives for the long term?
- Who do you want to visit your site?
- What solutions or benefits can you offer to these visitors?
- What data should your site provide to achieve your primary goal?
- What information can you provide to encourage them to act right now?
- What questions do you get asked the most on the telephone?
- What questions and comments do you hear most at trade shows?
- What data should your site provide to achieve your secondary goal?
- Where does your target audience look for information?
- How often do you want visitors to return to your Web site?
- What may be the reasons you don't sell as much as you'd like to?
- Who is your most astute competition?
- Does your competition have a Web site?
- What are ways you can distinguish yourself from your competitors?
- How important is price to your target audience?

Your answers should indicate which competitive advantages to stress, what to show, what to say, what to feature. Serve your content in bite-sized pieces, all valuable — clear, current content leads to success on the Web. If it's a winner for your guests, it will be a winner for you.

37

As with most other marketing endeavors, publicizing your site will help increase its value to you and the rest of the world. Unlike offline promotion, online promotion is far more under your own control.

For instance, you can access PRWEB at www.prweb.com and use this free resource to post your own press releases. Also, the VirtualPROMOTE site at www.virtualpromote.com provides free resources for promoting your site.

Publicity will bring the news of your company to the world, whether they're online or not, whether or not they even have computers. The basic weapons you'll need are a press kit, a company background piece, press releases, story ideas, articles or columns about your firm, and press demonstrations.

The press kit includes the background piece, press releases, photos of your executives or your products, story ideas, reprints of previous articles about your business, a list of customer references, and anything else that the news media might find newsy. Understand that *they need you more than you need them,* providing you furnish them with news that will appeal to their readers.

Examples of such news are your online presence providing new convenience or lower prices, special information that can only be obtained about you online and not offline, any product or service you are offering for the first time, even the fact that yours is the first business in your community that now makes its offerings available in cyberspace.

Study the media outlets you use now and the type of stories they run. Think of how your story will fit into their makeup. Do the same thing for TV and radio. Almost everything about the online world is still new and exciting for many people, so capitalize upon the momentum already generated by the Internet. There are also a host of online magazines that might want to post your story, so find the news in it and send it to them.

Begin your publicity campaign with a master plan. Long before you even put your site online, recognize the key messages you want to send your prospects about your company, the online and offline publications in which you want those messages to appear, and specific ideas for articles. The more newsworthy you make your company, the more coverage you'll get. And publicity will earn credibility that advertising just can't buy. Your goals should be uniqueness, timeliness, and awareness. Remember that without publicity, a terrible thing happens: *nothing.*

38

Online guerrillas *have many potential allies in cyber-space*. Many of them want to help you, to team up with you — and most importantly — want you to help them. This happens when you trade links with them. Your site calls attention to them and their site calls attention to you.

This form of marketing partnership can attract many visitors to your site, each visiting not because of the money you've invested online but because of the friends you've made. Not linking is not thinking.

To find appropriate online marketing partners with whom you might trade links, think in terms of connecting with companies that have the same kind of prospects and standards as you. Guerrillas engage in a weekly surf to locate potential partners. When you find them, you won't enter into a long-term arrangement, but a short-term relationship to see if everything works out for both of you. So don't think marriage. Instead, think fling. If it's fun, you'll do it again.

Got a banner on your site? Put it on another site in exchange for your returning the favor to the other site owner. You'll discover raftloads of exchange opportunities at Free Banner Exchange — netfreebies.hypermart.net/freebann.htm. Many online marketers will be delighted to scratch your back with a link or banner if you scratch them same way. As you may have learned, there's a lot of back-scratching going on in cyberspace. The old phrase to describe this method of marketing was "tie-ins." Then it was called "collaborative marketing," and then "co-marketing." Guerrillas then called it "fusion marketing," and today all these phrases refer to "trading links."

Go to your favorite search engine. Mine it for the names of potential online marketing partners. Consider your own community, your own chamber of commerce. Go to local listings and get listed yourself. Do online research within your own industry and you'll find a wealth of people who didn't even know they were guerrillas till you phoned them or sent an e-mail suggesting the idea.

Tell them that linking helps spread their exposure in cyberspace without adding a penny to their costs. Tell them that we're in an interdependent age and that networking is invaluable for small businesses.

Use software that enables you to track the number of visitors to your site who come from the sites of your partners. You don't want to cover your site with links, but you don't want to miss out on all that free visibility. The idea is to reach a state of perfect balance, linking your way to the bank.

39

One of the many reasons to include online marketing in your modus operandi is because *you can do so much of it for free.* Cyberspace is teeming with opportunities for guerrillas to prove their marketing mettle by investing much of their time, energy, imagination, and cybersavvy instead of investing much of their money, if any. Never in history has commerce been so friendly to the business without the funds to match its dreams.

Your participation in bulletin board services, also known as forums and newsgroups, costs nothing. Your attendance in targeted chat rooms costs exactly the same. Classified ad opportunities galore await you, many of them free. Visit www.getrealproductions.com/adlinks.html. You'll discover a long list of classified advertising sites at which the cost to market is nil.

One of the most endearing qualities of e-mail, ranking right up there with speed, is its cost. You can have an aggressive, continuing guerrilla online marketing attack using e-mail, forums, classified ads, and chat rooms for less than the cost of a pack of gum. You can offer 24-hour-a-day, 365-day-a-year convenience, locations just a mouse click away from any wired place on earth, and provide lightning-quick service without paying for these privileges (beyond the nominal monthly online service charge).

Limitless opportunities exist for you to host conferences, publish articles, give demonstrations, pen a column, and conduct surveys. Those surveys, by the way, are not only free, but are superb chances for you to generate information that garners free publicity. Set up a survey at your site — without programming — by visiting SurveySez at www.surveysez.com.

It will cost you nothing to write and disseminate online press releases — even your press kit is very close to free. The testimonials you'll display at your site don't cost a dime. And the research you can accomplish with your own online focus groups or through the universe of data online costs you not a thing. With your e-mail campaign, the stamps are even free. The playing field is tilted in favor of the guerrilla.

Did I mention linking as a free online marketing weapon? Did I mention partnering with online allies with whom you can conduct special online events such as conferences and celebrity appearances? Even the promotion of your online presence offline rarely involves more than the cost of a line in all of your printed and electronic marketing. *Free enterprise exists at its freest in cyberspace.*

40

The biggest problem with online marketing is how it is perceived by many business owners, who believe it to be an automatic income producer. That belief causes them to create Web sites and e-mail addresses, then sit back with the expectation that prospects will find them and place orders. Online marketing is not the miracle worker many believe it to be.

You must know the territory. It's very different from the terrain in which you've been operating. Not only must you know the intricacies of search engines, but you must take advantage of what you know — actively and daily — and keep up with a marketing medium that is changing every day. All of your competitors aren't dummies. Many of them are mining cyberspace for your prospects, your customers, your opportunities.

To succeed online, you must know that cyberspace's *essence is action, its promise is speed, its most fertile opportunities are in its interactivity*. It calls for activity on your part if you want activity on the part of your prospects. It calls for blazing speed in response time, for warmth in a cold electronic world.

Nobody on earth knows that you're online until you tell them. And even when you tell them, they're probably not paying attention, so you must continue establishing your online presence, continue keeping up with the technology, continue resisting the unnecessary bells and whistles found in abundance online, continue staying at the leading edge when it comes to providing information to your prospects and customers, and continue dazzling them with your luscious Web site.

As with other media, you must be clear and on target, aggressive and patient, follow-up-minded and people-oriented, consistent and ethical. But unlike with the other media, you must also be attentive and curious, fresh and current.

Online marketing is really an invitation to guerrillas to work harder, but in a new direction, capitalizing on opportunities that have never existed before, many of which they can dream up by themselves. Old-fashioned marketing required an investment of money and could foster a lazy attitude. Online marketing requires a minimal investment of money, but demands an attitude of action, alertness, and attention. It can work wonders; however, it cannot do the work for you or without you. It helps with the job of marketing but does not do the job. That's your task. This is the most important fact about online marketing.

CHAPTER SIX

INSIGHTS INTO DIRECT RESPONSE

41

irect response marketing is very different from indirect response marketing, although guerrillas like it best when the two are teamed up. The first is geared to obtain orders right here and right now. The second is geared to obtain orders in the future. Although a fair amount of standard, indirect marketing is usually necessary to set the stage, to make prospects ready to buy, and to distinguish your company, it's direct marketing that will lead you to taste blood.

As you well know, we are living in the age of information. Most information is easy to gather. However, information is not insight. It's the combination of information and thought that leads to insight, and it's insight that will make you a standout in the direct response arena.

The first point is that *direct response marketing either works immediately or not at all.* Unlike standard marketing, which changes attitudes slowly and ultimately leads to a sale if you go about things correctly, guerrilla direct response marketing changes minds and attitudes instantly and leads to a sale instantly if you go about things correctly.

When it works, you know it. You don't have to wait months for your message to penetrate the mind of your prospect. Your time-dated direct marketing offer either results in a sale right now — or it doesn't.

To succeed with direct marketing in any medium, remember these important facts.

1. Your offer is omnipotent. The best presentation in the world faces an uphill battle if you make a weak or ordinary offer.
2. The market to whom you direct your message can make or break your campaign. The right message delivered to the wrong people will result in no sale.
3. What you say and how you say it is easily as important as to whom you say it. Talk in terms of your prospects and how your offer benefits them.
4. Carefully account for every cent of your campaign to reach maximum profits. This requires as much creativity as your message. Guerrillas excel at this.
5. The more often prospects have been exposed to your other marketing vehicles, the more readily they'll accept your direct marketing offer.

Some principles of indirect marketing apply to direct marketing. You must still talk of the prospect, not yourself, and you must make a clear and cogent offer. But from that point on, direct marketing is a whole new ballgame. And it's one that you can win with the insights of the guerrilla.

42

S tupid mistakes in horrid abundance have been made by otherwise bright companies when testing the direct response
waters. Fortunately, guerrillas can learn from these blunders.
To list them would take an endless series of books, but I will
provide insight into ten of the most notable blunders.

- Failure to attract attention at the outset dooms many brilliant
  campaigns before they have a chance to shine. Envelopes, opening lines, mail subject lines, and first impressions are the gates to
  your offer. Open them wide.
- Make a direct marketing explosion. Do not relegate your attempt to the ordinary, which means the ignored. Guerrillas say
  things to rise above the din, to be noticed and desired in a sea of
  marketers.
- Focus your message on *your prospect*. If you focus your message on yourself rather than your prospect, your effort is wasted.
  Prospects care far more about themselves than they care about
  you. So talk to them about themselves.
- You must know *precisely* who your market is. Research into
  pinpointing that market will be some of the most valuable time
  you devote to your direct marketing campaign.
- Telephone and mail to only honest prospects; otherwise you

waste your time and money. If you make your offer to people who don't really have a need for your offering, it will be an incredibly tough sale.

- Initiate direct-response marketing with specific objectives. Begin by creating the response method for your prospects so you'll know what your message should say.
- Stress your benefit before you feature your price. If you feature your price before you stress your benefit, you tell prospects what they don't want to know yet. Your job is to first make them want what you are offering; then you can tell them the price.
- To concentrate on your price before your offer is to waste a powerful selling point. Even if your price is the lowest, people care more about how they'll gain from purchasing. State your low price at the right time.
- Failing to test all that can be tested is a goof-off of the highest order. Test your price points, opening lines, subject lines, envelope teaser lines, benefits to stress, contact times, and mailing lists to know the real winners.
- Setting the wrong price means you've failed in your testing and your research. Guerrillas are sensitive to their market and their competition. Test prices and constantly subject them to the litmus test of profits.

As direct response vehicles become more sophisticated and prolific, guerrillas *zero in on the exact people to contact,* so as not to waste time or money on strangers. Successful mailings to strangers net as high as 2 percent response rates. Successful mailings to customers and qualified prospects net up to 10 percent and even higher. Precision leads to profits.

43

After you have researched your market, industry, competition, media availabilities, pricing, and benefits that you'll highlight, you are ready to create direct-response materials. Once you've compiled the critical intelligence, it's time to generate your own materials.

The materials you create may be for direct mail, mail order, print advertising, direct-response television, direct-response radio, telephone marketing, postcard decks, door-to-door salespeople, home shopping TV shows, catalogs, Web sites, trade shows — any method of marketing that attempts to make a sale right then and there. It does not require a middleman.

Although direct marketing appears to be a one-to-many marketing situation, it works best when it feels like one-to-one marketing. Don't forget, even though *you may mail to millions, they read or hear your messages one at a time.* That insight alone can boost your response rates.

No matter which method you'll use to direct market, you must still gain attention at the outset. You must still talk in terms of the recipient. You must still respect both their time and their intelligence. And you must still make an offer that's just too juicy to refuse. Technology is influencing the venues in which you may reach out to your market, the speed at which you may impart information, and the ease of accepting your offer, but in the end, direct response marketing is more about people than things.

Therefore, when you state your message, you must prove you know that people still matter the most. Create marketing materials that will earn prospects' trust and confidence but won't brutally erode your budget. Always offer value regardless of price, and be aware that your competitors are knocking themselves out courting your prospects and customers. They may be using technology even better than you are. But who are they more interested in — themselves or the people they're romancing? I know where your priorities reside.

It is incredibly difficult to actually motivate a human being to alter their behavior to the point where they want to put out their hard-earned money for what you are offering. But it happens every day. And although the growth of direct-response marketing and the growing number of options make the job appear more challenging, the practical savvy of the guerrilla makes it easier. After testing copiously, guerrillas know exactly what to do.

In the mind of the inexperienced direct marketer who has plunged into the process without the proper homework, there are many options. In the mind of the guerrilla who has prepared, there are few.

44

I f you embrace the concept of tweaking, you will dramatically improve the results of your direct-marketing campaign. Great campaigns don't usually hit the center of the target; instead, they come close to the target, and then your tweaking moves them ever closer to the bull's-eye.

Tweaking means that you devote energy to finding a better mailing list, a more cogent message for your envelope or mail subject line, a still better way to state your message. The more research you continue to do, the more you'll learn what customers love about you — and about your competition. This tweaking will add firepower to your messages.

The best tweakers are the experimenters. Although they may have a winning direct-response campaign, they are constantly testing other markets, other messages, other direct-marketing methods, tweaking here and there to build their direct-marketing muscle.

We all know that great things rarely happen instantly, and this includes the direct-marketing campaign. Even the best have to be tweaked or they atrophy with time. The sense of urgency that is so necessary for direct marketers becomes less immediate with repetition. Where repetition is crucial for mass marketing to take hold, it is of lesser importance in direct marketing. Certainly, offers may be repeated, but the line you don't want to cross is a lot closer than you think in this arena.

The most successful direct marketers play an endless game of increasing not only their response rates, but more important, their profits, with each marketing effort they make. Their primary ally is not their budget but their desire to tweak, to improve, to break records

Records are made to be broken, not to serve as a permanent standard. That means change is part of the game in order to steadily increase profits. It means new records are being established on a regular basis, not because of major new marketing campaigns, but because of minor improvements on a consistent basis. Guerrillas are not defeated by failures in their experimentation, merely enlightened.

Customers are changing, and guerrillas are keeping abreast of their new wants and needs, their expectations and hopes. The marketing tools that worked like a miracle last year may be losers this year. That direct-mail campaign that generated so much profit last year may be surpassed by that Web site you create this year. But these marvelous things aren't going to happen because of a flash of genius. Now you have the insight to know that *they'll happen because of tweaking and experimentation.*

45

t's hardly a secret that radio and television are lethal weapons in the arsenal of a direct-response-minded guerrilla. But few small businesses are aware of the low cost of testing these hyper-powered media for direct response. Be not intimidated by these mass media just because you're a small business. *They're not as mass as you may think and both can help generate higher profits than you may think.* This fact is crucial.

Instead of measuring your CPM, your cost per thousand viewers or listeners, as traditional marketing had dictated, measure your CPO, your cost per order. If you drum up $10 in sales for every $5 you invest in TV time, you're doing very well. Every guerrilla alive will gladly invest $10,000 in TV or radio time to generate $20,000 in sales.

However, watch the stars in your eyes. From that $20,000 you must subtract your TV time, the cost of your product, the cost of TV production, your cost of doing business, and any other money you've laid out to earn those $20,000 in sales. What's left over are your profits. If you don't have any money left over, you need a lower CPO or a different price.

Although it's true that the Internet will surpass radio and TV for measurable commerce, radio and TV are marketing mainstays because you can be certain they'll produce profits for you if you can meet specific criteria.

To get off to the right start, your margin should be in the 500 percent range. If it costs you $20 to make or buy, you ought to be charging $99.95 in the offer you make on the tube or the radio. Your product must have mass market appeal, especially to the blue-collar, middle-class segment of the public. The uniqueness of your product will help it succeed, and if you can demonstrate it in action, you'll be using TV in the best way possible.

Although the number of products marketed on radio and television grows each year, the following products have been most successfully marketed in those media: books, videos, health and beauty aids, CDs, exercise equipment, housewares, mattresses, and products oriented specifically to the channel on which you're marketing, such as golf clubs on the Golf Channel.

Your commercials must take firm hold of your viewers' or listeners' emotions. Offerings centered around fear, greed, glamour, and sex sell the best. Of course, you must accept all credit cards and allow buyers to make periodic payments. Every single word you say must be devoted to making that sale at the time the audience sees or hears it. Delays are fatal. Show and tell your toll-free number proudly. If you test and fail in three tiny markets, the cost will not hurt you. If you test and succeed in those same markets, you can expand nationally and reap lush rewards.

46

Because of technology, which ensures a low cost of production, and because of the Internet, which ensures a wide range of availability, increasing numbers of guerrillas are discovering the joy of marketing by catalog. And you can post your catalog on the Internet. It used to be that the idea of a catalog for marketing was reserved for the big guys with the big bank accounts. My late father-in-law could affirm this, for he published the Sears catalog for several years. However, you can do now what he did for Sears then.

You can publish a catalog using your own computer: you can then mail it to precisely targeted lists or you can publish it on the Internet. People will use search engines or links of your allies to find you. When they do, they'll discover they can not only learn about you, but also browse through your offerings, select what they want, and place their order.

Although many catalog companies no longer even publish a paper catalog, my mailbox still teems with them every day but Sunday. Many are tucked into my newspaper that day. And the names on them are not the names of loser companies. The same catalogs appear on a regular basis, and when you see the names of successful companies on regularly mailed catalogs, you begin to see that if you can *center your business around regular customers*

— and that's the insight you must have — a catalog can make you wealthy.

You must speak to your customers as though you know exactly what is on their mind and that you share their concerns. Treat your best customers especially well, lavishing attention and sending freebies and personalized messages to them. *Never* take them for granted.

Many of the old rules about catalogs are out the window now because of the Internet. You can invest money in small media ads that call attention to your Web site and disseminate your catalog online to those people who take the time to visit your site. Encourage them to sign up to receive your catalog regularly. Sending it by mail is pricey. Sending it online is priceless. The more attention you devote to making the most of the Internet with your catalog, and vice-versa, the more you will use this extraordinary medium to your best advantage as a catalog marketer.

Although many of the old rules have changed, many of them still apply. Your product must be perceived as an excellent value. You must show and tell enough information for prospects to make an intelligent buying decision. You must make it extremely easy to order. And you must make it irresistible to buy from you right now.

47

Guerrillas are fully aware of the proliferation of direct-response marketing in the world today. They see it on their computer monitor, in their mailbox, on their telephone, on radio, on television, on signs, and in the magazines and newspapers they read. Guerrillas know that *it is more difficult than ever to make their snowflake stand out in the blizzard.* There are countless other snowflakes out there, each enticing and hoping for attention. Each one competes with yours because it insists on attention, money, time, and a meeting of the minds. How can you make your snowflake be the one that starts the avalanche of thought that leads to a sale?

You need to understand your prospects' minds. What do they read or watch? What are their foremost interests? You can be sure that what they respond to captivates their interest.

You can captivate prospects' attention by making your offer so fascinating to them that they are truly enticed. The offer should focus on your prospects, not you. And it must stand apart from the other offers being made to them on a continual basis.

But even if it is too good an offer to pass up, how can you be certain it will get their attention?

It must be unique to their eye. If it looks like all the other direct-response pleas, it will be tossed or ignored just as they are.

Ninety years ago, you could have simply mailed a letter. But today, because so many companies mail letters and grab for attention, you must go about your business differently.

Guerrillas accomplish this by using alternate modes of delivery, unique graphics and colors, precision timing, brutal honesty, emotionally charged verbiage, and a tangible sense of one-to-one communication. They never waste their prospects' time. Guerrillas direct their marketing to the center of the bull's-eye. They never try to say everything to everybody, but concentrate instead on saying something to somebody.

They study what their competition is doing and then do it better. They research the direct-response tactics that are working for others and then adapt these tactics to their own needs. They experiment with technology. They learn from their customers exactly what motivated them to buy. Research and patience help their snowflakes weather the storm.

48

O nce you have the rapt attention of your prospects, you're only part of the way to your destination. You must now make these good people desire what you have and recognize that it will make their lives better in some way, that it is worth any money that you ask for it, and that the ideal time for them to own what you are selling is this very instant.

Your offer must be so tempting that it is clear to them they are best off if they accept it. How can you make this kind of offer? It must have three elements if it's to be an offer that's easy to accept.

- Your offer must be clear, for regardless of the other details, if they don't fully understand it, they're not likely to accept it. Many offers are clear only to the marketer making the offer and not to the prospects.
- Your product must be obviously beneficial to prospects in terms of bettering their existence, whether it be their personal or business lives. Prospects will be attracted to your features, but their hearts will be won by your benefits.
- Your offer must appear as a solid value. Many prospects are not necessarily interested in a low price or even the best price, but all of them want a great value. And many of them love low numbers, so partial payments will appeal to them.

Some of the best offers are those that extend free trials, because they eliminate any perceived risk in buying. If you have enough faith in your offering, it's worth an effort to test this tactic. Offers that expire within a brief time are also more likely to be accepted, especially if the price is clearly a bargain. Offers that carry the promise of a free gift when the offer is accepted fare better than the same offer without the gift. First-time offers are better than stale offers, but it is true that many marketers have learned that their offer must be made more than once.

One marketer, a nonprofit organization, learned that the response to their second mailing, identical to the first, generated nearly the same response rate as their first mailing. They also learned that a third mailing was a financial disaster. It's important to know when to quit, but all markets aren't the same — so you'll have to experiment to learn your own limits.

The first company to make the offer you're making stands the best chance of having that offer accepted. You must *connect your offer with something that already exists in your prospects' minds*. The closer the connection, the more likely the sale.

49

I t's going to be tough for people to say yes to your offer if they've never heard of you, if you haven't established credibility, if they're not entirely confident in your business.

Some firms try to shortcut that mindset by making spectacular offers, and sometimes those offers are accepted. The vast majority of the time, however, people do not choose to transact business with a stranger. And to most people in the universe, you're a stranger.

You can address the identity issue by using other marketing strategies that set the stage for your direct-marketing offer. When people read about you in magazines and newspapers, hear about you on the radio, or learn of your company in other media, they become conditioned to accept what you offer. You have distinguished yourself from the ranks. You have entered the domain of familiarity.

It is invaluable for you to know how *familiarity bridges the gap* between "I've never heard of you so I'm reluctant to accept your offer" to "I've heard of you and trust you and so I'll accept your offer."

Familiarity develops over time. You become recognizable because of your marketing vehicles and, most of all, from the marketing vehicles in which you'll be making specific offers. So if you'll be doing a mailing, begin to attract attention with postcards or a brief note before going for the jugular.

Many guerrillas employ the "two-step" process. The initial marketing offers a free brochure or video, softening up the prospect for the sale. That's step one. Then they move adroitly to step two, where they ask for the sale — using a letter or phone call. Because of the valuable information they've provided, the sale is easier to nail down.

The process of establishing loyal customers begins with the prospect learning of your existence. It moves to the stage at which the prospect respects your company. Then the prospect wants to learn more about you, finds that he or she can, studies your marketing materials, and finally realizes that you are trustworthy and offer products or services of unimpeachable quality. Then the prospect is ripe and ready to say yes to your offer.

This is the point at which you should strike. If you attempt to make a sale before you have earned their confidence, you have a very good chance of failing — even with a marvelous offer. Guerrillas don't take that risk.

50

I n 2001, direct-mail marketing alone is projected to produce $346 billion in sales to individual consumers and $238 billion in sales to businesses. That pie is too big and juicy for guerrillas to ignore. That is why they carefully study the successes of other direct marketers. If guerrillas become students of what has worked in the past, they will be fully prepared to live in the past — so they must blend the best of past direct-marketing successes with the best that the present has to offer. The past taught them little about Internet marketing or fax marketing.

Guerrillas know that the public of today has seen it all, done it all, and probably purchased the T-shirt. So how can they tell the winning direct-response campaigns from the losers? They have the insight to look for *repeat* mailings, mailings that are not lampooned.

Most important, they do not operate on gut instincts. Instead, they test and never stop testing. They well know that marketers such as *Time* magazine, which has been using direct marketing for decades to sell subscriptions, has tested hundreds of letters and TV commercials, paying as much as $15,000 to have a letter written. Yet they continue to test each year because big numbers are involved in direct-response marketing, and fractional increases often make the difference between enormous profits and dismal failure.

It's always important to remember the power of the word "free." In a test of three offers — all at the same price — observe the power of "free." Offer one was for one year of service for $99 and the second year for $10. Offer two was for two years of service at a 50 percent discount. Offer three was for one year at the regular price of $109, and the second year free. It was offer three that received 40 percent more results than the other two.

Thomas Edison said, "Many of life's failures are people who didn't realize how close they were to success when they gave up." Guerrillas interpret this as a call to test, to tweak, and to learn from the success of others. Because they refuse to give up, they rarely stop short of success. They know that the path to it is well trodden if they know where to look.

CHAPTER SEVEN

INSIGHTS INTO PEOPLE

51

You certainly don't need me to remind you that marketing is far more about people than it is about things. So the more you understand and truly do love people, for each is fascinating, the better equipped you are to market to them. You're fairly well equipped already, because you're a person, so you have a lot in common with your target audience. But every guerrilla must exhibit these ten character traits.

- You must be *patient* enough to allow your marketing to take hold and soar. It doesn't happen overnight, but it does happen if you have the fortitude to hang in there. Most business owners just don't have it.
- You must have the *imagination* to use the media to their best advantage, to see how technology can help you, to wade through the marketing clutter and create ways for your message to come shining through.
- You must have the *sensitivity* to see things from your prospects' and customers' point of view and from the perspective of your competitors. The more sensitive you are, the more profits you'll net.
- You need the *ego* to stand up to the people who love you, but who give the worst marketing advice: your coworkers, employ-

ees, family, and friends. They tire of your marketing long before your audience does.

- You need the *aggressiveness* it takes to use a wide range of weapons and outmarket your competition. In 1998, U.S. businesses invested 4 percent of gross sales in marketing. You are more aggressive than that.

- You need the desire for *constant learning* that will keep you strategically positioned in the marketing arena. Marketing options are changing faster than ever. Keep up with them!

- You must be *generous* with a penchant for giving things away for free if they can help your customers, especially imparting information. Giving opens wide the roads through which getting flows.

- You must be *energetic* because of the constant attention required by marketing — attention to maintaining, tracking and improving it regularly. Only high-energy people can devote the proper attention.

- You need to be a *people person* so that you can understand what's on the mind of your target market. Many business owners are oriented to things and ideas more than people, but people are your interest.

- Maintain your *focus*. If you lose it, your marketing campaign will grow weak. It is difficult to stay concentrated in the face of daily distractions and temptations, but your focus will be a potent ally.

52

A s you are aware of the chemistry of successful guerrillas, you must also know the chemistry of *customers*. Today's customers are far more sophisticated about marketing than ever. They know all the tricks and have fallen for some of them — so their radar is keenly attuned to scams.

The American Dream is first for financial security, then for home ownership, followed by having a family, holding a secure job, and being happy. Great marketing helps customers achieve their dreams.

Your prospects want to know how you'll solve their problems. They are looking for ways to simplify their lives, to reduce the stress that is part of daily living, and to patronize businesses that share their values, such as protecting the family, honesty, stable relationships, self-esteem, freedom, friendship, and respect for one's ancestors.

Customers want to buy products or services that are linked with a cause, even if it means paying higher prices. They use their emotions to help them visualize themselves benefiting from a purchase from you. Now more than ever, buying decisions are based on emotion. So guerrillas relate each benefit they offer to a particular emotion.

Customers do business only with firms that have earned their confidence, established credibility, are recommended by their friends, make believable claims, and offer freedom from risk with a powerful guarantee. They buy from companies that provide convenience, display respect for them, and exhibit a style that matches their own style. They buy neatness and clarity. They buy your reputation.

Customers do not buy fancy adjectives, exaggerated claims, clever headlines, special effects, marketing that screams or hints of amateurishness, highly technical marketing, industry jargon, the lowest price anything, unproved items, or gorgeous graphics that get in the way of the message. They do not buy from Web sites that keep them waiting.

They also do not buy humor that hides benefits, offerings heralded with unreadable type, poor grammar or misspelled words, salespeople who don't listen, or things they don't fully understand or trust.

People respond to marketing that involves prospects and informs customers. *They want long-term, caring business relationships.* This insight will help you to stand apart from your competitors and shine in the minds of your prospects and customers.

53

Your prospects are similar to you, except that they're probably doing business with one of your competitors. Fortunately for you, that competitor most likely doesn't know the full meaning of follow-up, leaving customers feeling ignored after the sale.

These are among your hottest prospects. They already do business with a company such as yours and may be disenchanted because they've been left alone after making their purchase. That's why guerrillas identify their best prospects and then begin the courtship process. *It is a courtship and it is a process.* Armed with that insight, you can transform them into customers.

Most business owners contact prospects once or twice, and if they don't show an interest, the business owners move on to greener territories, on to the nonexistent Land of Instant Gratification. Guerrillas continue romancing those they are courting. Eventually those prospects feel so cared for, so important, so attended to, that they switch over and begin to patronize the guerrilla who never stops courting.

How long does it take? Try seven years on for size. That's the outside. It could happen in a month, even a week or less, if the prospects are in the market right now and neglected by their former supplier. But it probably won't happen soon and it most assuredly won't happen if you ignore them after contacting them once or twice. Many guerrillas aim to secure only the consent of their prospects to receive marketing. After the consent and more wooing comes the eventual sale along with the concomitant repeat and referral sales.

Remember that prospects have minds that are more open than you think. Allegiances are lost every day, allegiances are gained every day. When guerrillas speak to prospects, whether in person or through one of the venues of marketing, they do not talk about their businesses or their industries. They talk about the prospects themselves — which is the topic most on the mind of prospects and the one that ceaselessly interests them. When a guerrilla can talk to a prospect about the problem that person faces, the guerrilla gains even more attention.

Guerrillas need to talk about solutions to their prospects' problems, seeing things from the *prospects'* point of view. As weeds are flowers whose beauty has not yet been discovered, prospects are customers who have not yet realized all that you can offer them. Give them time. Give them information. Give them attention. While you're waiting, walk a mile in their shoes so you can be better prepared to talk to them about how their feet feel.

54

People patronize businesses for an enormously wide variety of reasons. Often it's location, though the Internet is changing that in a hurry. Frequently, it is mere habit. Guerrillas know in their bones that the prime reason is the buyers have confidence in the sellers. That is closely followed by the quality of the offering. And next comes service — which guerrillas know should be defined as "anything the customer wants it to be." After service comes selection — and again the Internet rears up as a contender for business because of the staggering breadth of its selection. And fifth comes price. To some people (fewer than 20 percent), price is the number one criterion. But those attracted by price make the most disloyal customers because they're easily wooed away by somebody offering a still lower price. *Guerrillas build their businesses on loyal customers.* Guerrillas have the insight that they must do all in their power to maintain loyalty.

You can maintain customer loyalty with frequent-buyer programs, with special events centered around customers, with fervent follow-up, with a newsletter, with little freebies for your customers. Most important, recognize the customer and use his or her name, talk about personal things before getting down to business, listen very carefully and sincerely to what your customer is saying. Listening is considered one of the most crucial parts of follow-up. It's no surprise that people patronize businesses that listen to them.

Many marketers create their marketing under the ridiculous assumption that prospects are asking "Who are you? What is your product or service? When are you open? Where are you located?" The only real question in the prospect's mind is "Why should I care?"

Here's what your customers want: it's not "Tell me a story about you." Instead it's "Tell me a story about me. Tell me how you can save my time, increase my income, reduce my stress, bring more love into my life, cause people to think highly of me." If you can't talk to them about these things, leave those prospects alone, for you're wasting their time and your money.

People patronize businesses that can offer things to change their lives for the good. Sometimes these are huge things, such as cars and computers. But usually they're not. After all, how much can a new shirt or a new paper stock for stationery change a life? Not much, but you've still got to be thinking in those terms.

Keep in mind that people are attracted to businesses that have established credibility. You build credibility with superb marketing and commitment to a plan. Marketing continues to be a blend of art, science, business, and patience.

55

The single most important insight for the new millennium is to *reach out for your customer base.* To rank near the top is to engage in as much one-on-one marketing as you possibly can. Attesting to that is the hottest application for an Internet site — chat sessions. People love the one-on-one aspect of it, so that even though millions of people are online, many of them are engaged in one-on-one conversations. That alone is probably the biggest reason for America Online's unparalleled success.

I remind you of the Internet's unique ability to provide one-to-one communication. By using e-mail, it's fast and easy to carry on a dialogue with your prospects and customers. Of course, you can also do it at trade shows, on the phone, in person, and by mail. But faster and easier is the net.

Guerrillas know in their hearts that every customer is an individual and wants to be treated as such. Through customer questionnaires, guerrillas learn of their customers' individualities. Although there are tens of thousands of names on your mailing list, your customers want to be serviced and sold to one at a time.

One-on-one marketing is akin to having somebody whisper in your ear rather than shouting across the street, as is the case with mass media marketing. One-on-one marketing allows guerrillas the chance to cozy up to customers, to customize their marketing, to increase the delight factor of doing business with them.

The essence of the guerrilla's joy — long-term relationships — is found in one-on-one marketing. Guerrillas know well the enormous difference between their customers and their best customers. This enables them to treat their customers like royalty and their best customers like family.

To engage in one-on-one marketing, they must market with absolute precision. They must know their best customers from the rest, then market to them in ways that prove they care. Guerrillas tailor their relationships to helping their customers succeed at whatever they wish to succeed at. They do all they can warm up relationships. And they play favorites.

Keep in mind the true tale of the nonprofit organization that increased its response rate 668 percent by treating its biggest donors in a special way — special but not expensive. They mailed to them a letter requesting funds and enclosed the letter in a handwritten envelope using a commemorative stamp. At the end of the letter was a twenty-five-word handwritten note. Hardly fancy, but astonishingly effective. It's not quite one-on-one, but it gives you the feel of one-on-one marketing in action. It's the wave of the future. And to guerrillas, it's the wave of the present.

56

The psychology of marketing requires basic knowledge of human behavior. Human beings do not like making decisions in a hurry and are not quick to develop relationships. They certainly do want relationships, but they've been stung in the past and they don't want to be stung again.

They have learned well to distrust much marketing because of its proclivity to exaggeration. All too many times they've read of sales at stores and learned that only a tiny selection of items were on sale. They've been bamboozled more times than you'd think by the notorious fine print on contracts. And they've been high-pressured by more than one salesperson.

That's why they process your marketing communications in their unconscious minds, eventually arriving at their decisions because of an emotional reason, even though they may say they are deciding based on logic. They factor a lot about you into their final decision — how long they've heard of you, where your marketing appears, how it looks and feels to them, the quality of your offer, your convenience or lack of it, what others have said about you, and most important, how your offering can be of benefit to their lives.

When a customer states that he or she wants to buy your product or service, you can be sure that the customer was guided by his or her unconscious mind. The consistent marketing of your benefits, your message, and your name has penetrated the sacred unconscious mind. Prospects come to feel that they can trust you and so they decide to buy.

Any pothole in their road to purchasing at this point might dissuade them. They call to make an inquiry and they are treated shabbily on the phone? You've lost them. If they attempt to access your Web site for more information and can't find it or find one littered with self-praise, you've lost them. If they visit you and feel pressured or misunderstood, they're gone.

You've got to realize that the weakest point in your marketing can derail the strong points. Excellence through and through, start to finish, is what people have come to expect from businesses, and these days they won't settle for less. *Marketing is a 360-degree process,* and you must work on your agenda from all angles at all times. When it comes to marketing, your prospects have built-in alarm systems, and any shady behavior on your part sets the bells to clanging, the sirens screaming.

It is very difficult to woo a person from the brand they use right now to your brand. Although they are loathe to change, they do change. And when they do, they patronize businesses that understand the psychology of human beings and the true nature of marketing.

57

Guerrillas strive for and savor long-term relationships with their customers. They well know the myriad benefits of long-lasting connections and do all in their power to establish and nourish them. They're well aware that it costs them six times more to sell something to a prospect than to sell that same thing to a customer.

It's one thing to know the value of a long-term relationship. It's something completely different to engage in activities that spawn such delicious connections. The chemistry of a long-term relationship is as complex as the chemistry of a long-term and happy marriage.

The starting point is your commitment to the happiness of someone else. The next point is a goal not of customer satisfaction, because that's relatively simple and common, but of customer bliss — exceeding the expectations of customers, giving more than they anticipated, caring more than they're used to sellers caring.

To do this, you have to learn about them. You learn first by listening to them, then by asking more questions and listening carefully once again. Guerrillas often ask questions on their Web site or with prepared customer questionnaires that solicit personal information. If you know your customers' personal likes and dislikes, you can render personalized service, such as clipping articles of interest and sending them to special customers or recognizing their achievements and the achievements of their families or businesses.

Handwritten notes on mailings make customers feel singled out. Phone calls that are not part of a telemarketing campaign accomplish the same. Using the customers' names, talking with them of nonbusiness topics, alerting them to special new products or services you have available, and responding instantly to their calls and e-mails, faxes, and letters — all those seemingly insignificant actions act as beneficial catalysts in the chemistry of a healthy buyer-seller relationship.

The more details you know of your customers' lives and businesses, the more empowered you are to mention those details, making each customer feel unique and special rather than part of a large demographic group. *There is an extraordinary chemistry that exists in long-term relationships.* They don't always happen instantly. But when they do, the business owner is as delighted as the customer. Guerrillas know that no two customers are exactly the same and no two customer relationships are exactly the same. Like marriages, all are different and all can be mutually rewarding.

58

Many a hard-working, well-meaning, marketing-minded business owner will sabotage their business with ill-advised marketing. That's even worse than no marketing because bad marketing is incredibly expensive.

Ill-advised marketing is usually the result of a personality flaw in the business owner. The most common flaw by far is impatience. So many entrepreneurs are dazzled at the prospect of instant gratification that they grow impatient and then begin a new marketing campaign, never giving the first one a chance to take hold and soar.

Another all-too-common personality hang-up is an ego the size of Alaska. Business owners figure that they know finance and they know management, and therefore they know marketing. Not true. They may know marketing as it existed when they embarked upon the road of individual enterprise, but you and I know how much marketing has changed since then. Often, their humungous egos motivate them to write their own marketing copy, design their ads and Web sites, and select media based on their personal tastes rather than the tastes of their prospects and customers. Those egos often beckon them to become their own pitchmen in the mass media. Sometimes that works. Usually, it blows up in their kisser.

Another personality blemish that puts marketing on self-destruct is the ridiculous notion that word of mouth will do the trick all by itself. And then there's the crazy companion notion that your prospects already know all the reasons why they should do business with you.

Want to know another nutty personality defect possessed by the losers? They think they simply can't render better customer service than they're presently providing. Don't ever think this thought. There is always room for improvement. Just ask any customer. Ask them, perhaps with your questionnaire, how an ideal business such as yours would be run. Be ready for true enlightenment when they tell you.

Of course, conceit ranks high on the list of personality blotches — the conceit to think that people want to know all about you right off the bat, that they care about you more than they care about themselves, that their time is your time, and that they don't know amateurishness when they see it. And still another impediment to marketing success is being too good a consumer. Such business owners fall prey to fast-talking media reps and buy things they don't really need. Or they spend too much on the production of their marketing materials. Remember always that *there is no marketing strategy strong enough to withstand the personality of a clueless business owner.*

59

There's an old adage that says that it's better to know something about your spouse than everything about marriage. Same is true for marketing. Guerrillas have gobs of information about their customers because if they didn't, their marketing wisdom would be for naught.

Marketing is like a pipe with the guerrilla on one end and the customers on the other. It does not exist in a vacuum and it does have a goal. To reach that goal, it is essential to gather personal data about each customer. It is somewhat helpful to know your customers as a group, but it's more helpful to know them individually.

Gain information by talking with them, listening to what they say, sending them customer questionnaires, visiting their Web sites, meeting them at community events and trade shows, and making yourself available to them for any dialogue they wish to initiate.

An important insight is that *the more you know about individual customers, the better you are able to tailor your marketing.* As you custom-tailor it, the marketing becomes more effective and economical at the same time. Instead of sending a mailing to all of your customers, you mail to only those customers who you know will be interested in what you're now offering. By doing so you cut down on your cost while increasing your response rate.

When you know specific customers are interested in baseball or opera, you can send them tickets to such events — or gifts that connect with their interest. When you read of them or one of their family achieving something that's worth publicity, you acknowledge the achievement with a call or a note. How many huge companies can do that? That's one of your advantages as a small, customer-centered business.

Knowing details about your customers enables you to connect with them and adapt your conversations with them to their own personality types. If they are Type A people, always in a hurry, that's your cue to keep it short and do it quickly. If they are deliberate, studious, now you know to give them all the facts they need and not speed through your presentation.

Personal knowledge about individual customers enriches your customer list exponentially. You know what they like, what they read, what they watch, what excites them, what turns them off, where they shop, how they perceive your business, tiny details that make the difference between a one-time buyer and a lifelong customers. Best of all, guerrillas have fun learning that information, connecting with other people with the goal of mutual satisfaction.

60

Hardly anybody becomes a customer by accident. There is usually a lot of intent involved. Your intent is to gain and keep them as customers. Their intent is to find a seller who they can trust, who is convenient, who provides value, and who has exactly what they need.

That's not all they look for. They also look for easy availability of information. You grant that with your Web site and marketing materials you've created, such as brochures, catalogs, or a newsletter. They look for credibility. You provide that with the professionalism and constancy of your marketing. They look for their friends' opinions. You benefit from positive opinions because you have an active referral system, a file full of testimonials, and you know how to gain word-of-mouth recommendations in addition to using the net for word-of-mouse referrals. They look for care and attention. Your fervent follow-up accomplishes both.

The real insight is that *buyers look for sellers who give more than is expected.* When I mention customer bliss, I'm hoping you'll render service and offer quality that makes customers totally satisfied rather than just plain satisfied. Those who feel total satisfaction are six times more likely to repurchase during the next eighteen months than those who are merely satisfied. And totally satisfied customers are the most loyal.

Buyers want you to listen to them, to act upon what they say, to make the entire act of purchasing a positive experience for them. The more you can save their time, they more they'll appreciate you.

The idea of giving buyers exactly what they seek in sellers begins in your own head. You've got to want to transport them to the Land of Customer Bliss. You've got to want lasting relationships and act as though you do, so much that they can't help but sense it.

Do it with eye contact, a smile, use of their name, a customer account number, free gifts, special prices, follow-up reports, a newsletter, handwritten notes, free information of value, and rewards they never expected. Remember those baseball or opera tickets?

Customers are looking for a lot more than you're selling. Know the best predictor of preference for McDonald's? It's not their fast hamburgers. It's their clean restrooms and good French fries. Clean restrooms are the main reason women select the gas stations they patronize. Customers want things other than what you sell. Your job is to find out exactly what. That's not so hard if you've got the love of people possessed by guerrillas.

CHAPTER EIGHT

INSIGHTS INTO ATTITUDES

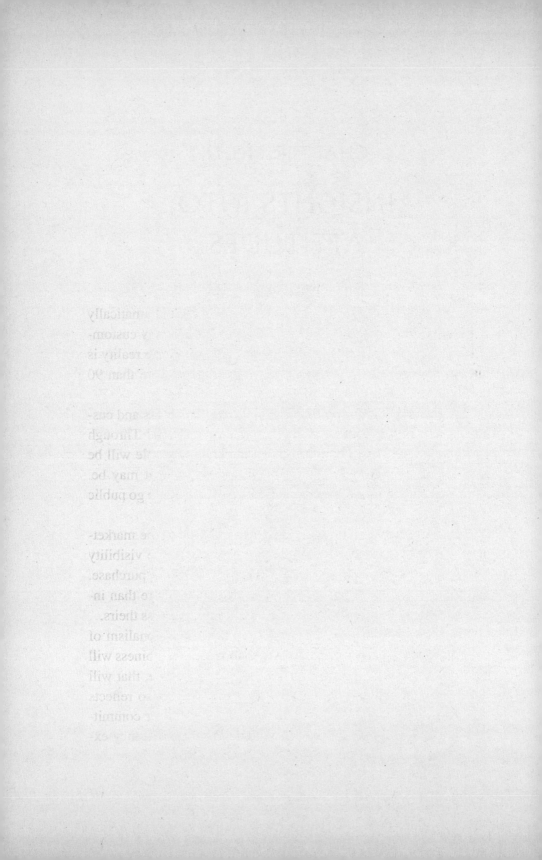

61

The attitude of a guerrilla toward marketing is dramatically different from that of a nonguerrilla, which is why customers of guerrillas feel blessed to be customers. The reality is that 90 percent of life itself is attitude. And even more than 90 percent of marketing is attitude.

That attitude is probably the first thing your prospects and customers will notice about you. How will they know it? Through your marketing. If you don't do much marketing, people will be unaware of your attitude regardless of how winning it may be. Private attitudes do not equate with profits. You've got to go public with your attitude.

Let people sense it through your aggressiveness in the marketing arena. It will be clearly communicated through the visibility granted you by marketing. When it's time to decide on a purchase, they'll be drawn to companies with an attitude far more than invisible companies that don't actively and proudly express theirs.

Your attitude will also be indicated by the professionalism of your marketing materials. If they look shabby, that shabbiness will become part of your attitude. If they inspire confidence, that will express your attitude. The reach of your marketing also reflects your attitude and so does the frequency. Naturally, your commitment to your program conveys an attitude. Your consistency expresses it as well. Keep switching your media and message, your niche and format, and people will be unclear about your attitude, assuming you're not even sure of yourself.

Of course, you can't succeed on attitude alone. On the other hand, sometimes you can. Marlboro may not be the best tasting cigarette in the world, but it certainly has the right attitude. Same for Budweiser. Many product category leaders succeed with attitude more than excellence, attitude more than low price, attitude more than lavish spending. Every car made can get you from point A to point B, but some do it with a more stylish attitude.

You must have the insight to know that *your attitude must come shining through in all of your marketing.* It will come across by what you say, how you say it, where you say it, and how frequently you say it. Even the world's most winning attitude is for naught if it's not being transmitted. That's why guerrillas communicate with a big attitude to compensate what they lack in a big budget.

62

An attitude that is mandatory if you're to be a guerrilla is outwardness. Inward focus works against you when it comes to marketing. Save that for your analyst's couch, and shine your light outward-bound when you're marketing.

The insight you require is the knowledge that *your marketing is not about you.* It is not about your business. It is not about your product or your service. I hope you're clear on that because if you're not, you'll blur up the other insights necessary for you to master guerrilla marketing.

There is always a very good chance that what you have to offer will mean a lot to your target audience. And there's a small but real chance that it will mean a great deal to them right now. Those simple facts ought to mean a lot to you before you plunge headlong into a marketing attack. If you can adapt your mindset to just what your offering can mean to your prospects, you're thinking properly.

If you've got the right attitude about marketing, you're nearly fixated on providing your customers with precisely what they need. One of the things they do need, as do all members of humanity, is a sense of identity. If you operate from the inside of their minds, you'll be able to make yourself part of their identity. The fact that they do business with you and have a lasting relationship with you will become part of their identity and it will be very clear to their colleagues and friends.

Since your attitude is centered around your customers, other facets of your business will follow suit. Your service will pick up and customers will notice. The people you hire will share your attitude, and again, customers will notice. The way you run your business will never seem stale to them because of your innovation in delivering customer bliss.

If you can see the future before it unfolds, you have an immense competitive advantage. Without a doubt, the best way to engage in customer-oriented marketing is to continuously innovate and to be the very essence of flexibility. In the past, it was common to stick with the tried and true. Today, however, you must focus on your *customer.* "Business as usual" now means "business as unusual." If you're to be a guerrilla with the right attitude, look at situations from your customers' point of view, then meet and exceed their expectations. Know where you're headed, what your competitors are doing, and what your prospects and customers are thinking.

63

'm certainly not going to indoctrinate you into the teachings of
Zen Buddhism now, but I am going to suggest that you begin
thinking of your marketing in a very zenlike manner. Zen itself
simply means "living in the moment." It reveals to you the scope
and majesty, the size and importance, the preciousness and opportunity contained in each moment.

Guerrilla marketers are *fully cognizant of all the implications of
the moment.* They have the perception to realize its promise. They
are aware of the moment, each one as it passes. They are aware of
the possibilities it offers, but also of its fleeting nature. If they do
not capitalize on each moment, then each will pass, never to return
again in exactly the same way and in the same situation.

Capitalize on each moment by directing your core competency
in marketing to where it can do the most good for your customers
and prospects. Know the significance of timing, and never allow
the right times, the right moments, to be wasted.

Your prospects are prepared to buy for only a moment. They
make their final purchase decision, after processing it over a period
of time, in just one moment. And your marketing attack, to be
carried on for eons, begins with a single moment, like the first step
in an endless race.

Guerrillas know in their hearts that luck is what happens when preparation meets opportunity. You do all in your power to offer excellence across the board in your operation. You put out the word with your active and pervasive marketing. When that inclination toward excellence intersects with that penchant for putting out the word about your business, you get lucky and attract business. The preparation took a long time, the word-spreading took a long time, but the intersecting took only a moment.

When you create signs that connect with your other marketing or engage in direct mail and advertising before making telephone calls, you're paving the way to that blessed moment of purchase decision. The process that leads to the magic is a time-consuming one, but the magic occurs in a moment. The magic moment of marketing is a familiar moment to guerrillas.

Virtually all that you do in marketing must be directed to the moment of purchase. Respect each moment your customer is indeed your customer, and you will gain the benefits of their follow-up business and their referral power. Remember that reality is the architect of all magic moments in marketing.

64

I t seems a bit unreal to consider your attitude about being organized as an attitude that leads to successful marketing. But the better organized you are, the more your marketing will be able to flourish. Being organized also means being neat. The premises at your store, office, home-based business — wherever customers may visit — speak eloquently about your business, whether you like it or not.

Sloppy premises signal to prospects that if they ever experience troubles with their purchase from you, they'll be treated the same as the premises — in a messy manner. If they sense cleanliness all around them, they'll unconsciously assume that you run your business the same. If your premises are tidy, you don't run a Mickey Mouse operation. Best case in point is where Mickey Mouse resides — in Disneyland. An attitude of neatness and tidiness is so all-encompassing in Disney parks that everybody notices. The Disney people have always been blessed with the insight that *clean surroundings indicate you run a smooth organization,* that customers will be treated carefully, and that everybody enjoys a pleasant purchase experience. Employees at Disneyland clean the restrooms every half-hour. They know it's not pleasant to be in places that are not neat.

Neat premises are the outcome of a positive attitude toward

marketing, an attitude that is not assumed only on Monday mornings, but that influences employee actions every single second your business is running. As with most guerrilla marketing attitudes, this one costs no money — only time and energy, and the awareness of the importance of neatness.

Being neat means being organized so that you can render better, speedier service. This attitude helps prevent you from investing precious time looking for lost items, on investing money if you can't find them. It motivates you to create systems for tracking, communicating, ordering, updating, remembering important details.

Not many marketing people realize the close association between neatness and profits. But that association does exist. You would be positively appalled if you knew how many people refuse to patronize a business in which they've spotted sloppiness — in the physical space of the office, on the phone, in the communication, in any of the myriad manifestations of marketing. Don't think your customers don't notice breaches of neatness. They do. And they show their displeasure by never gracing your premises again.

Now that you have this insight, it's crucial for you to convey it to everyone who works with and for you. Neatness is only as neat as its sloppiest component. If you're a guerrilla, there won't be any sign of untidiness.

65

Every business book author writes about enthusiasm. Every business book author writes about passion. This business book author is no different. Enthusiasm fuels the fires of marketing, and passion is the highest expression of enthusiasm. This enthusiasm, which should be borne of product knowledge, must be honest, fervent, and apparent. It automatically arises when you're genuinely excited about what your offering can do for your prospects, what it has done for your customers. It is the healthiest contagion in the world today. Sincere enthusiasm arises in the heart of the business owner, then spreads to the employees, the marketing allies, the customers, and then to their friends and associates. Everybody who senses it catches it if it is direct from the heart. They want to be in on the excitement; they want to become as enthusiastic about your offering as you are.

The insight you must have is that *your job is to make them enthusiastic every way you can* — with the fire in your manner as you communicate with them, with the light in your eyes as you describe how their lives will be enriched from your offering, in the omnipresence of your marketing. The fire burning within you does not make itself known by high pressure or sentences that end in exclamation marks. It emits its warmth by your confidence, by your guarantee, by your focus on what it can do rather than what it is.

A very pious man lived on a flood plain and the skies opened, raining down upon him and his house. When the water rose to his knees, a boat came by and offered him a ride. He turned it down, explaining that his faith in God would save him. The water then rose to his chest, and another boat came by, imploring him to get in because the water would continue to rise. Again, he disdained the boat, stating that his faith in God would prove to be his salvation. The water continued rising, now reaching his upturned chin. Amazingly, a helicopter flew into view, then hovered above the religious man, lowering a ladder to take him to safety. He waved the helicopter away, again professing his belief that God would deliver him from harm. The water continued rising, eventually drowning the man. After his death he went to heaven, where he saw God. He asked why he wasn't there to save him in his hour of need. God said, "I'm almost positive that I sent two boats and a helicopter."

Your boats and helicopter are in this book and in your heart. You must believe so much in your product that your hallmark is passion.

66

You have more allies in the quest for effective marketing than your own enthusiasm and passion. True, they will serve to provide a built-in momentum to your marketing, but there are other sources that can help you: you have many other people who will rally to the fore to empower your marketing and your dreams. These allies come in all forms and exist in far more places that you may imagine. *These people actually want to help you. All you have to do is enlist their aid.* You must do so not only with words, but also with your manner and with good deeds that you perform for them.

The first allies to consider putting onto your exact wavelength so that they generate their own passion and enthusiasm for your success are your employees. They might look like employees to you, but you've got to see them also as marketing partners. Each one should gain as you gain, should act on your behalf because it is in their own best interest as well. Each one is a valuable member of your marketing team and should identified as such.

Your customers are also potent marketing allies. They'll be delighted to carry you banner forward into the fray if you allow them to experience customer bliss. They also must be asked, must be told of the importance of customer referrals to you. Be honest and be forthright when asking.

The Internet is the source of countless potential allies for you. Furnish links to their Web sites from yours in return for their returning the favor. Just be sure they have the same kind of prospects and the same lofty standards that you do. Help them and they'll be motivated to help you.

Earlier I mentioned the idea of fusion marketing — putting up signs for other businesses at your place in return for their doing the same for you, sharing the cost of a marketing expense because it increases your marketing exposure, but does it economically because you're sharing the cost. Your fusion marketing partners are ideal allies. They want you to succeed because they like you, trust you, and know you want them to succeed. We no longer live in the age of the lone wolf entrepreneur. We now exist in an interdependent society. Guerrillas succeed because they get a little help from a lot of friends.

Your marketing allies might also include some of your key suppliers, competitors from far away, local businesses serving the people you serve, even large national corporations that are well aware of the need for allies. They might even include your banker, your local chamber of commerce, or your landlord. The more allies you have, the more poised you are to succeed. Remember, they exist all around you.

67

Guerrillas render exceptional service, but that's not what makes them so special and that's not what their customers really notice and point out to their friends. Instead, it's that guerrillas want to render extraordinary service. They do it not because it's in their service manuals, but because it's in their nature, part of their DNA.

You can be certain that such an attitude is necessary for the best kind of service, the kind that assures each first-time customer will become a long-time customer. Guerrillas look for this trait and hire people who possess it. Anyone can train an employee to render wonderful service, but it is very difficult to train an employee to want to render such service. You've either got it or you don't and guerrillas search for those who have it.

The insight to incorporate is that *personality dictates the quality of service.* Some people are born helpers, desiring to help others no matter what it takes. Companies that have employees with helper personalities have a head start in the superlative service department. Their employees revel in delighting customers and giving more than is expected, and they do it not for the money but for the joy in helping.

Today's customers feel *entitled* to first-rate service, so you must surpass first-rate and take your service to an even higher level.

You've got to remember always the only definition of service: it's anything the customer wants it to be. Less than anything is inadequate service. L. L. Bean believes "customer service is just a day-in, day-out, ongoing, never ending, unremitting, persevering, compassionate type of activity."

Compassion is the key. You use it when you market to customers, trying to see things from their point of view. You use it when you service those customers, your radar keenly attuned to their needs and wants.

The rule about service is not golden — it's glittering: do unto others as you pray they will do unto you. Is there any correlation between spectacular customer service and long-term customer loyalty? You tell me. Guerrillas know that being the kind of person who truly enjoys rendering service requires a thick skin and a warm heart, an ability to listen and to be resourceful, to be empathetic and patient, to be assertive and quick to laugh. It's not a piece of cake to find such people or even to be such a person, but in no instance do I tell you that guerrilla marketing is easy.

Who will set the tone for the exquisite service you will provide? You will. Always keep in mind that all customers are not created equal and that guerrillas match the best service to the best customers. Your effort to make them feel wonderful should be part of your bottom line. That's where you'll see it reflected.

68

You have a lush opportunity to communicate your attitude when you're networking in social situations. You not only have the benefits of making eye contact, being able to smile, shaking hands, and proving your listening ability — you also have the chance to form the human bonds that must exist in order for a firm business bond to be forged.

At networking functions, which guerrillas attend with both peers and prospects, you can ask questions, listen carefully to the answers, focus on the problems of people with whom you're talking, and prove that you really are tuned in to those people, one by one.

The insight that gives guerrillas an edge while networking is that *people care far more about themselves than about you,* and if you allow them to speak about themselves, they'll remember you and like you.

Many business owners attend networking functions trying to pass out as many business cards as they can, while guerrillas try to collect as many business cards as they can. Other business owners see such functions as chances to blow their own horns. Guerrillas see them as chances to listen to the music from the horns of others.

Each gathering you attend is another opportunity to transform strangers into friends, to convert prospects into customers, to take the first steps at establishing strategic alliances, and to stand out in a sea of sameness.

Guerrillas do not try to meet everybody at such gatherings. Instead, they try to meet some people and get to know them. They realize there is very little that substitutes for warm personal contact, and hardly anything that can take the place of actually proving that they listen and care.

For all marketing techniques and plans, follow-up enriches networking. For instance, when you meet a prospect, you should actually go as far as to take notes about what that person said, then write a brief letter within forty-eight hours quoting something the person mentioned. How better to prove your conscientiousness? How better to stand apart from shallow contacts?

The essence of guerrilla networking is sincerity, warmth, and the ability to see the fascination in others. Everybody is interesting. Everybody has a story to tell. Everybody wants to be heard. The key is to discover what makes them interesting, to get them to tell their story, to listen and think of ways you can make their lives or their businesses better. In most of business, you are marketing your product or service. While networking, you are marketing yourself.

69

You already know that people do businesses with those firms that have gained their confidence. You also know that the river of confidence runs along a streambed of credibility. The meaning is clear: you must convey an attitude that gains credibility for you.

The insight is that *every bit of your marketing either builds upon that credibility, detracts from it, or does zilch for it.* Knowing that, you must adopt an attitude that reflects credibility for your business and yourself.

Like it or not, your credibility will be influenced by the tone of your voice, the clothes that you wear, the way your phone is answered, the look of your marketing materials, the places those materials are seen, your ability to keep up with the times, your stationery, your business cards, absolutely everything communicated by you or members of your business. That means all your associates must also act in ways to gain credibility.

Think of exactly what prospects experience when they are in the market for what you sell. First, they may ask around to get recommendations. If you don't have credibility, you're not going to be recommended, for your lack of credibility will reflect adversely upon the person who could speak highly of you. Next, they may try to remember anything they've ever read or heard about companies offering what you're offering. If you lack credibility, there's not much likelihood of their remembering you.

Perhaps they'll consult the Yellow Pages. That's where you're probably surrounded by competitors. Does your ad have the most credibility of all the companies advertising there? You're a goner if it doesn't. Prospects may scour the newspaper for ads offering what they want. They will not be swayed your way if your ad doesn't inspire credibility. If they call your firm, your credibility is enhanced or undermined by the way your phone is answered. Tiny details serve as the foundation for admiration and trust.

Perhaps you can say in your ads, "as seen on television," or you can say in your TV spots, "as seen in the *New York Times*." Perhaps you can say both on your Web site. Do you have a large collection of testimonials? If you do, lean upon them because they give you credibility. Can you quote facts and figures that foster credibility? If so, quote them. People do not want to have experiments blow up in their faces; they love to know that others have done the experimenting for them.

An attitude that establishes and nourishes credibility should be apparent in all your marketing, every customer contact, everything you do in the name of your business. The more the credibility, the higher the profits.

70

Everybody and his cousin does strive in their own way for credibility. They see things from their customers' standpoint as well as they can. They have an honest enthusiasm about their offerings. They try, in most cases, to prove they're a together company by attending to business neatly and keeping their premises as tidy as possible. They do what they can to get their employees pulling in the same direction they are pulling. They try to render service, although frequently it ranges from subpar to merely adequate. They network to the best of their ability.

With all those other businesses waving their arms, trying to call attention to themselves, how do guerrilla businesses stand out? Easy. They are fully aware of the competitive situation and they avoid any hint of me-tooism. They prove their uniqueness by the manner in which they connect with prospects and customers, by their patience, by their attentiveness to detail, by realizing that everybody who does business with them is a person first and a prospect next.

You can stand apart if you exceed the expected. Lavish personal attention on your customers. Learn the special knack of making each person who contacts you feel unique and special.

Stand out and be committed to innovation. Welcome change. See the inherent individuality in all your relationships. Have no sacred cows in your ways of doing business. Everything can be changed when necessary, when advisable, when the going gets tough. To stand out, you must examine every facet of your business with an eye toward not only improving it, but *constantly* improving it — your marketing, your service, your quality, and your relationships.

Guerrillas are never too sure about things. They are on a permanent quest for excellence and uniqueness. Because they take nothing for granted and know that their competitors want to succeed as much as they do, they pay very close attention to those competitors and constantly try to surpass them.

They know they're in a race and they realize that nobody is standing still. If they do, at least one competitor and probably much of the world will pass them by. They do everything they can to avoid sameness and to recognize the difficulty for prospects of selecting a business to patronize. How can they be selected? By their attitude of wanting to be exceptional.

CHAPTER NINE

INSIGHTS INTO TECHNOLOGY

71

The very first thing you must know is that *technology isn't what it was when you were growing up and isn't what it was when I was writing this sentence.* The blurring speed of change in technology is so pervasive and dramatic that only a dunce would attempt to pin it down. Breakthroughs are reported every day and happening at a pace even faster than that. Your job is to be aware of the changes and to be grateful for technology.

Yesterday I was watching my football team getting thumped on television. Both teams had wireless technology connecting coaches and assistant coaches, spotters and analysts, and it was all working like a charm. But my team was seriously losing. I made a note then to remind you now that it doesn't really matter how good your technology is if you're not very good. My team could have had even better technology, newer and faster, and still would have had their derrieres whipped. The effectiveness of your technology will reach as far as your own effectiveness and can't surpass it. If everything else is equal, the business with the best technology will win out. But if you have the best technology and not the best attitude and strategy, you haven't a chance.

To make technology your ally, the first thing you need to do is learn to love technology — not for what it is, but for what it can do for you. The greatest advances in technology in the '90s were not the lower costs and increased power, but the simplicity of using technology. User manuals are more clear than ever, and the technology itself is far more user-cozy. Technology gives small businesses an unfair advantage: it allows them to appear as powerful as the big guys without having to spend big bucks. Technology has not only leveled the playing field, but has actually tilted it in favor of the guerrilla.

That means doing everything you can to increase your comfort level with technology — taking a course, enlisting the aid of a consultant, reading a book, going to seminars and practicing. How do you get to Carnegie Hall? Practice, practice, practice. How do you get to love what technology can do for you? Practice, practice, practice. It's hard to break a computer, so your mistakes won't hurt you — unless you don't risk making them.

The main idea is to learn what kinds of technology are out there to help you run a smooth operation, then to get what you need rather than what you want. If you fail to embrace technology, the world will pass you by.

72

Companies that have enlisted the aid of technology, made it part of their everyday business, have several marketing edges over their competitors who are lagging behind. By becoming virtual, which is a fancy way of saying "connected," they are able to use technology to keep in touch with their offices, their employees, their customers.

Guerrillas become virtual by means of their computers, to be sure, availing themselves of the speed of e-mail. They are also granted virtual status by means of their communication devices, such as cell phones, laptops, pagers, answering devices, and call-forwarding service. Guerrillas can be anywhere they like and still be available at a moment's notice when they're needed. *The better you're connected, the more you're available,* and the more you're available, the better you can run your business and serve your customers.

These days, technology is very visible and portable, thanks to wireless technology. How many people do you see each day walking down the street talking on their miniaturized telephones? Cellular phones allow people to engage in multiple tasks — such as conducting business while driving. Cell phones and laptop computers increase their efficiency while reducing their worktime — people can now put their business in their pocket or purse, so to speak. Many entrepreneurs have been able to save substantial sums on office rent by closing the office and carrying it with them!

The way to think is *digital*. That means connecting, wherever you are, with real data, tracking all customer interactions, and mining for even more information to better transport those customers to a state of bliss.

Let me urge you never to use your technology to bug your customers, to send junk e-mail to anyone on earth, to invade people's privacy, to be intrusive in any way. Digital power and virtual convenience are extremely easy to abuse. Never require customers to give personal information. Ask for it, but never demand it. Technology enables you to gather information without asking for it. If you purchase books from Amazon.com, you can then get recommendations about other books from the site: their technology enables them to review your purchasing history and then advise you on books you'd like.

However, guerrillas must take heed: when you do have information, use it judiciously. Don't bombard people with marketing materials.

As with all marketing, the prime beneficiaries of your technology should be your customers. When they appreciate your virtuality, your technology, and they let you know — you're using it right.

73

A few days ago, I received a flier from the company from which I buy my coffee. The owner called me to ask what I thought of it. I told him I loved what he was saying about delivering coffee to my front door, but asked why he didn't mention his Web site along with his phone and fax numbers. He said that his Web site didn't work, so he dropped it. I told him that most Web sites aren't successful because most businesses that have one don't use it properly.

A site that works reflects a combination of art and science. The art is to attract viewers to your site and to maintain their attention. If your site is attractive and engaging, you'll have succeeded at your art. Now, it's time for the science. The science is knowing what your site should accomplish for you, creating one that does just that, then promoting your site all over the place.

Many entrepreneurs put far more time into creating their site than planning what the heck it's supposed to do and how they'll advertise it so prospective customers will know it's there. On the Internet, people *scan*. They don't read. They don't hang out. If they don't see what interests them or if they get lost or cut off, they're a mouse click from being history.

To ensure that your prospects can find you, you must know your way around search engines. You should use keywords that identify your business, not merely your name. A newspaper in San Francisco might use its name, but would also use keywords such as San Francisco newspaper, metropolitan news, California newspaper, or even San Francisco Bay Area. To promote your site, which is *essential,* submit it to several search engines. Submission is an *ongoing* task, not a one-time shot. Next, list your site in hundreds of Web directories, where your site can be included in your information category. Many are available to you at no cost.

On your site, post pages that are smaller than most and with less text. Long pieces belong lower in your site rather than at the beginning.

Linking with other sites, running interactive banner advertising on high-traffic sites, e-mailing to people who are likely to be interested in your products and services, and becoming an integral part of related newsgroups are important ways to call attention to your site. Be sure to list your Web site on your business cards, printed materials, and all other marketing weapons, because the site does you no good if your prospects aren't aware that it exists. The insight: *Web marketing is a component of all marketing campaigns and must be integrated into the campaign* rather than existing on its own.

74

nformation increases in value the more you share it. Sharing it has never been as easy as now. Guerrilla marketers share their information freely, knowing that by offering it, they are establishing themselves as authorities. They disseminate valuable data in person at free consultations, by mail in the form of free brochures, in lecture halls where they conduct free seminars, in newspapers where they pen a regular column or occasional article on the topic of their industry, in club meetings where they give free presentations, and online where they host conferences and post articles on sites read by their prospects.

This information-sharing helps both the planet and the guerrilla. By becoming an expert — and sharing their expertise — they attract customers and begin to form bonds.

The sharing of information moved into hyperspeed with the growth of computer networking. Companies around the globe are able to communicate with each other and tap into data banks for the benefit of all — again, as with all guerrilla marketing — with the goal of helping their customers. Information-sharing puts all of your allies a mouse-click away.

If you enter a dark room with a lit candle and see that everyone else has an unlit candle, you can light all of their candles with yours, brightening the room without affecting your own candle.

Light other people's candles with your information, capitalizing on the *synergy!*

Guerrillas have the insight that *they have a lot to share.* They can establish networks and strategic alliances, entice prospects, help customers, and run a streamlined operation by sharing information, as you know, but also by sharing databases, files, plans, technology, management skills, customer service, workspace, purchasing power and marketing clout. They can share personnel, capital and creativity.

You must develop a radar for what you can share, who you can share it with, and how you can do it. The Internet has changed business forever by making it so simple and fast to collaborate, disseminate, and enlighten.

Be careful not to spread too much information, too many details. In the information age, data is gushing toward people's brains like a firehose aimed into a teacup. You should impart information of value, but be selective in whom you share it with, what you share, and where you share it. In the past, information was carefully guarded, but the past is history and the future holds the most promise for those who light the candles of others.

75

Credibility, customers, and cost-effectiveness. Those are only three of the advantages granted by the kind of technology that enables you to become your own marketing firm, your own advertising agency, your own production studio, your own printer. Software exists that makes these complex tasks simple, able to be handled with aplomb by even the most inexperienced entrepreneur.

Because that software changes and improves, is updated and revolutionized so rapidly, no book that hopes to be timeless dare list it by name. The insight is in realizing that *now you can do for yourself what used to cost a lot of money,* take a lot of time, and often be created by the wrong people for the wrong reasons.

You don't even need creativity. All you require is a computer and the software that enables you to produce superb marketing materials at a tiny fraction of what they used to cost. Instead of dreaming up eye-catching graphics, all you have to do is select from an enormous array of graphics offered by your software, then click your mouse. You can create marketing weapons that, both please the eye and motivate the prospect.

Create your marketing weapons by incorporating technology into your growth plan. Add special graphics cards or accelerator cards into your computer to add muscle to your hardware capabilities. Use application software developed by companies other than the manufacturer of your own computer. Add high-storage memory cartridges to your computer to increase your current storage capacity. One of the main reasons that companies fail is because they are not able to manage the growth they've attained. Invest in technology with *optimism,* as your ability to use your computer will reflect how well you can manage your company's growth.

But always remember that no matter how much technology empowers your company, you're still living in an analog world. After all the e-mailing, voice-mailing, and faxing, personal contact will put you over the top. The more personalized you can make your communications, the more tailored to each customer, the better they'll fare and the better you'll fare.

In the past, marketing was relegated to experts. But today, guerrillas know in their hearts that their primary focus should be on their customers and not their experts. Making experts happy with your actions is not what you should be doing — making *customers* happy is your goal. Invite them into your business and be careful not to overwhelm them with an Internet labyrinth. Where you direct them to go, be certain they'll like it there.

76

O nce you have the proper software, the proper attitude, and the knowledge of how to use technology to create a winning marketing plan, all you have to do is decide on which marketing materials to incorporate as part of your guerrilla marketing attack.

Before you make these decisions, recognize that certain principles apply to nearly all of them. You must be clear as to what you want your prospects to do after they've received your communication. Your prospects will ask, "What's in it for me?" You must hold back and not say everything at once.

First, you must pay close attention to your grammar and spelling, for your misuse of them can undermine your most compelling offer. Do not allow typos, contradictions, or omissions to detract from your message. People notice these things. And you can't simply say what you have to say without telling people what they are supposed to do next. Include a call to action with all of your marketing materials. You may want them to call you. Perhaps you want them to visit your Web site, send you a fax, complete a questionnaire, come to your store, look for you at the trade show. If you don't tell them what do to, they'll probably do nothing.

Armed with this understanding, you can select the marketing weapons that you'll create in your own office. You should consider brochures, fliers, direct-mail postcards, letters, self-mailers, and coupons. You can open your mind to publishing a newsletter, online or offline. You can create your own Web site, powerful point-of-purchase displays, signs, presentations, and catalogs. You can produce a wide assortment of sales aids, including profit-producing flipcharts.

Many guerrillas use technology to produce interactive CD-ROMs, videos, audiotapes, and high-powered publicity campaigns. They are very aware of the power of technology when they create proposals. Often, the simple addition of a professional-looking proposal that combines color, graphics, and visual excitement is what will cause the prospect to see things your way and buy your product or service.

Computers can help you design marketing materials that get signatures on your dotted line. Sometimes these materials are as basic as a circular. Sometimes they're as basic as a multimedia presentation employing sound and sight. Creating those presentations used to be a bear. Now it's a pussycat. *You are living in a do-it-yourself world.* Guerrillas have this insight and they do something about it.

77

Now that you know all the things you can create with your own computer, with a little help from your software, scanner, and printer, direct your attention to another major benefit bestowed upon you by technology.

Guerrillas have the insight to recognize the *sheer power of database marketing,* an ideal weapon for any guerrilla. It allows them to dominate their competition by using their knowledge of their customers to deliver unique products, services, and communications. A solid database enables you to learn so much about your customers that you can create new niches, which in turn allows you to expand and deliver new offerings.

Look at your database and realize that each name is an individual, not a mass-market statistic. Because they are individuals, you can learn of their interests, needs, and desires, of their occupations, families, and dreams, of their problems and their perception of you and your competitors. If you have a customer who ordered printer paper from you two months ago, you can contact that customer again to arrange for a reorder. By knowing what your customers want before they know they need it, you can offer it to them before your competitors have even a clue. Make sure that your computer databases, which have both customers and prospects listed, are always current. The moment you learn something new about a customer or prospect, enter it in your database.

Guerrillas know that every sale to a new customer is the start of a potentially long and fruitful relationship over the long haul. Although there may be many names in your databases, you build that database one name at a time. Each database is a two-way street — an avenue through which you communicate with customers and through which they engage in dialog with you. Encourage them to tell you what's on their mind.

By studying your database, you can learn the traits and statistics that your customers have in common. It might be location, automobile ownership, magazine subscriptions, habits, or age. It could be health, family makeup, or previous purchases. You can focus on your best customers if you have a database.

In the past, these databases were kept on three-by-five cards. Today they're kept in computer files. And the cost is so low to maintain them that even the guerrilla with the tiniest company of all can cash in on database marketing. The goal: find out what your customers want, then offer it to them.

78

Mark Twain said he never let his schooling interfere with his education. Regardless of your schooling, there's little chance it covered what technology makes possible today. If you took a course in how computers can aid your marketing, the first insight you would have gained would be into *the profitability for you if you become savvy about e-mail.*

When you think of e-mail, don't compare it with snail mail because it's considerably different. In fact, it is such an improvement on old-fashioned mail delivery that the U.S. postal service now uses it, and today there is a lot more e-mail being sent daily than snail mail. For this, guerrillas owe a tip of their propeller beanie to Ray Tomlinson, who invented e-mail in 1971.

You can use e-mail in your marketing in ways that will make your customers delighted to be doing business with you. Guerrillas love e-mail but hate junk e-mail, known as spamming. Their affinity to e-mail is because they can deliver their messages instantly and to anywhere in the world if the recipients are online, as more and more of them are with each word I type. That means e-mail saves you time in communicating and money that you used to spend on postage. It can also help save our earth's trees because it is so delightfully paperless.

Each recipient can read your e-mail on screen or print and save it just as with a standard letter, which does use paper. But you don't have to print and save your e-mail, saving you the cost of paper and the convenience of space. Save it in your computer. Make copies as you need them. All your files and memos can be kept in one convenient location. Each one is dated and timed. Many experts feel that for all the great things about being online, e-mail is the most valuable of all computer applications.

E-mail also helps you save on the cost of courier service and faxing. You can use it to send brief messages or long documents, to send black-and-white communications or colorful, beautifully de-signed materials. It's easy for you and easy for the person who receives your e-mail. Who should that be? People who want to receive it, that's who. Find their names on your customer list, in the newsgroups to which you belong, in chat rooms where they're talking about your industry, possibly even your company. Although e-mail isn't free, because you need a computer and In-ternet connection, it's far less expensive than telephoning, mailing, or faxing. When using it, keep your message as brief as possible — people read computer screens differently than they do letters. Peo-ple go online to save time, and they don't want to waste time reading long things. As Thomas Jefferson said, "Never use two words when one word will do."

79

As glorious as e-mail may be, nearly as wonderful is the ability of technology to let you do research. As card-carrying members of the information age, guerrillas take full advantage of the research capabilities granted to them by their computer and the Internet.

They use the net to tap databases filled with information about their competitors. They visit their competitors' Web sites on a regular basis. They hang out in chat rooms where their competition might be active. They join newsgroups, the same ones their competitors have joined. They bookmark selected sites on the Internet and mine those sites for information.

On their own Web sites, guerrillas ask questions, invite e-mail, and solicit information from customers, explaining how the customers will gain better service if the Web site operator knows more about them. Makes sense. They avail themselves of the copious libraries available online and by CD-ROM. They are regular visitors to brand communities abounding on the Internet, each one centered around its own specific industry.

They all have the insight that *the more they know, the more creative they can be.* The more they know, the better equipped they are to compete. The more they know, the more they will prosper.

This is why you keep hearing that information is the currency of the twenty-first century.

Guerrillas study every forum in which their competitors may be marketing. This includes the online classified ads, search engines, electronic magazines, and discussion groups. A full 90 percent of job-seekers questioned in 1998 reported that they used the Internet for job-hunting. Of these, 72 percent said they used the net to research the firms in which they were interested. Almost everything is moving on-line.

Whether it's industry information, legal information, medical information, or any kind of information, it's now available online. Better yet, it's easier to find. And reference librarians, those precious sources of information in the past, are now precious sources of information for the present and the future — for they know their way around the Internet like nobody else. Bill Gates has referred to the Internet as "The Information Superlibrary."

Research, valuable as it may be for your firm, doubles in value if you engage in it regularly. Your competitors know the value of updating their sites. Now you know the value of visiting those sites on a continual basis.

80

You're aware, as all guerrillas are, of how technology can strengthen your marketing. You also must understand its limitations and the new advancements that are taking place at breakneck speed. Don't let these advancements overwhelm you. Very little becomes obsolete, but nearly everything becomes improved.

Technology, for all of its wonder, can also be a major distraction and a drain on your time if you focus on the technology itself rather than the benefits it can bring to your business.

Kim Elton, the author of *Net Benefits,* reminds us, "Business is life and life is messy. Like a kitchen sink full of dirty dishes, you know that when you've finally cleaned them up, someone will burn a tuna casserole and you'll be back in sudsy water up to your elbows with a Brillo pad in no time. But if the kids are growing up healthy and strong — and helping out with the dishes now and then — it's all worth the effort. Soon you'll get a dishwasher and you can shift the mess from the sink to the dishwasher. The dishes still have to be cleaned. The technology eases the labor and takes away some of the pain, but it doesn't relieve the duty."

That's the insight that I want you to take from this chapter. *Technology helps you do the job, but it doesn't do the job.* That's your task. To understand how technology can help you, it's not necessary to learn the technical jargon, the nerdy part of technology. But you must comprehend the impact of technology and the ways it can transform a squirt gun into a cannon.

To cash in on the transformation, you must be in close touch with your needs. Technology will help you meet them, and you must know how best to use the technology in which you've invested to get the maximum benefit for the money you've put forth. Recognize hype for just what it is and solid science for just what it is.

You wouldn't dream of running a business without using a telephone. The computer will be just as endemic as phones. Using technology will be as easy as making a phone call. It's already well in its way. The investment research company Robertson Stephens put forth this statement: "Communicating is becoming the primary role of computers after four decades of number crunching. We stand at a technology crossroads and are witnessing a technological metamorphosis. . . . In our opinion, computers, originally designed for number crunching and applied to computing tasks for nearly fifty years, will be used in the future primarily for communicating." The future is now the present.

CHAPTER TEN

INSIGHTS INTO ECONOMIZING

81

When guerrillas think of economizing, they don't necessarily think of trying to save money. What they do think of is how to get the absolute most from any money they've invested in marketing. There are two kinds of marketing — expensive and inexpensive. Expensive marketing is the kind that doesn't cover the investment guerrillas make in it, while inexpensive marketing pays rich rewards for the investment. *Economizing has nothing to do with cost; it has everything to do with results.*

To be sure, guerrillas adopt a philosophy of frugality and thrift. They know well the difference between investing in something disposable, such as paper and accounting services, and investing in something that's truly an investment, such as a telephone system or customer-tracking software — items they'd use on a daily basis. There's a big difference between these two expenses, so you won't be surprised to learn that guerrillas rarely waste their time and effort on relatively low-cost disposable purchases, but are willing to expend the time and energy to enjoy a large savings on a an expense that's really an investment in disguise.

The key to economizing is to think not in terms of purchasing, but in terms of acquiring. Open your mind to trading, sharing, renting, and modifying an existing item. You may want to learn a few skills so that you can do rather than hire. Desktop publishing software enables you to save a ton of money which is usually paid to pros.

Guerrillas are also keenly aware of those instances in which it makes sense to hire a pro. Amateurish-looking marketing is an invitation to disaster. You might hire a highly paid professional designer to give your marketing items a powerful visual format, then use your own staff members to continue generating marketing materials that follow this same format. Learn from any consultant you hire.

To economize means to *invest wisely.* Guerrillas test their investments on a small scale before plunging headlong into any marketing plan. They have no fear of failure, providing the failures are small ones, and know that even one success in ten tries means discovering a path to wealth and profitability. They know in their hearts that money is not the key to happiness or success, but that enough of it enables them to have a key made. Real frugality is more about priorities and results than just saving money.

82

O f all the ways to waste money, the most common way in marketing is to fail to commit to a plan. Untold millions have been invested in marketing campaigns that are successful in every way except for a lack of commitment on the part of the marketer. Guerrillas are blessed with the insight to know that *it takes time for an investment to pay off, and instant results are rarely part of the deal.*

To abandon a marketing campaign before it has a chance to flourish is to squander money in three ways. First, all prior investing in the campaign will have been for naught. Second, it will be necessary to reinvest to generate the share of mind that precedes a share of market. Third, marketing materials will need to be recreated.

Small business owners waste money in other ways as well. Many of them invest in research instead of doing it themselves. Others dare to commit to a campaign they haven't tested. Still others create marketing materials that must be updated regularly, rather than creating timeless marketing materials. When you state in a brochure that you've been in business five years, you must update that brochure next year. When you print that you've been in business since 1996, this statement will remain current.

Small business marketers also waste precious funds by investing in amusing marketing, funny marketing, even uproarious marketing. Marketing has an obligation to put money in your coffers, not smiles on the faces of your prospects.

The most common method of economizing is also one of the most overlooked — marketing to existing customers. It costs one-sixth as much to sell an item to an existing customer than to sell that same item to a noncustomer. The price of discovering and convincing likely customers is astronomical when compared with the price of doing the same with current customers. Database marketing has lowered the cost of guerrilla marketing, and yet some business owners fail to even try to make repeat sales.

Guerrillas avoid buying what they want and don't really need, don't fall prey to slick salespeople representing new and unproved marketing tools, avoid bad decisions by never making rash decisions, and constantly ask themselves, "If I didn't need this yesterday, why do I need it today?"

Economic errors often made by entrepreneurs are failure to negotiate, comparison shop, or use the net for pre-purchase research. Know exactly where every one of your dollars is going. The leaner your spending today, the fatter your cushion tomorrow.

83

For every error made by small business owners in the area of economy, there are an equal number of brilliant maneuvers that guerrillas engage in to save money, to get the most from the least. Although some of these are obvious, others aren't as well known, yet each can make the difference between red or black ink on your bottom line.

The three most obvious, naturally, are to recognize the extraordinary value of committing to a single marketing campaign, the necessity of using marketing for the reason it was invented in the first place — to sell what you offer — and the good sense of marketing more to customers than prospects. Practice those three economies and you'll discover that marketing works better than you thought it would and costs less.

To economize, understand that small is beautiful. Consider enlisting the help of consultants rather than ad agencies if you can't do the work properly yourself. If you want to go the ad agency route, realize that as a small business, assignments for you usually will be relegated to beginners at large advertising agencies but to top management at small agencies.

Remember the enormous power of repetition if you're faced with making the decision as to what size ads and what length commercials you will run as part of your advertising. Small ads and short commercials cost less so you can run more of them — repeat your offer more frequently, access the unconscious of your target market, spread the word in more venues. On your Web site, the fewer words you have on each page, the better your readership. Say a little on a lot of pages rather than cramming all the verbiage onto few pages. Even your marketing plan should be brief.

The more you learn about marketing online, the greater you can reduce your marketing investment because you'll be able to communicate with fewer but more qualified prospects, render even better service to customers, and avail yourself of the many opportunities to market for free — through e-mail, user groups, chat rooms, classified ad sites, column opportunities, and by hosting a conference.

The most important insight into economizing is to *recognize the true nature of marketing — it's a conservative investment.* It's conservative because it won't double your profits instantly even if you do it with expertise. It's an investment because it pays off generously after time has passed rather than at the very beginning. Unfortunately for money-strapped new businesses, marketing is most expensive at the very beginning. But that's not the time to hold back on professionalism. You don't have to create a complex marketing plan, but you simply cannot afford to make mistakes. If you can't do it right, don't make the investment. That's guerrilla economizing.

84

One of the most sensible and effective ways to save money marketing is to make allies of other companies and groups reaching out to your target market. Share marketing activities and materials with them. Guerrillas know this as fusion marketing and they practice it vigorously. *It allows them to disseminate their marketing message to more people while reducing the overall cost.* Very guerrilla-like.

Offer to include a flier for a cooperating business in your next customer mailing — in return, they can do the same for you. More people will be exposed to your message this way, and you don't have to invest in the cost of locating them. You'll also save on postage.

Guerrillas align themselves with a wide array of marketing partners because they have learned that if they select partners who have their standards and market to their kind of prospects, they will enjoy high visibility and heightened awareness without having to pay the tab for such benefits.

Nobody on earth would have known what I meant when I wrote the first *Guerrilla Marketing* book if I had mentioned the value of trading links. And yet the ability to do just that is one of the most significant ways that the Internet is a bonanza for fusion-minded guerrillas. They discover marketing partners in their community as well as across the globe, and they offer to trade links from one Web site to another.

Such an offer makes solid sense because Web sites need all the help they can get in attracting attention. They get that help in the form of a hyperlink: people merely click their mouses and then see your site before their eyes — and get it at no cost. It sounds too good to be true, and yet countless guerrillas will swear to its veracity.

Mastering guerrilla marketing entails investing the time to locate marketing partners who can help you market aggressively without having to spend money aggressively. It means thinking of ways you can cooperate with one another — through joint promotions, special events co-hosted by several businesses, public relations efforts, posting signs for one another, sharing mailings, and sharing the cost of media investments, such as magazine ads or television spots.

In time, you'll have a corps of allies, ready to reach out to increasing numbers of people, helping one another in the spirit of cooperation and high-energy marketing. By combining talents and desires, you'll be networking at the level of guerrillas. The winners? You, your allies, and your customers.

85

Television investments frighten many small business owners away. They still equate the cost of running a TV spot with what it used to cost when they were kids. They see celebrities and fancy special effects in TV spots and they know they'd never be able to afford such high-profile glamour.

These scaredy cats lack the insight that *the cost of running and producing television commercials is but a fraction of what it was in the bad old days.* Those were the days favoring huge businesses with bottomless bank accounts. But these are the halcyon days of small business, with media fragmenting into tiny, affordable pieces — especially in the area of cable television. And technology has lowered the cost of TV production to the point that, although you shouldn't produce your own spot, you can be fairly certain that your cable station can produce it — and do it well if you give them guerrilla guidance. You must furnish them with a script, perfectly timed — the words and pictures set in advance. Also, you must record the soundtrack — voice, music, and sound effects, if any — before you shoot the video so that it can be shot to match the words exactly. *Rehearse* so that there are no surprises. And shoot several commercials at the same time, since the equipment, technicians, and talent are on hand.

The power of the commercial comes from the power of the

offer, not from special effects or celebrity presenters. Its strength comes from the efforts of those who created it to motivate viewers to desire what is being offered, to see the commercial through the viewer's eyes, to be *effective* rather than clever. The cost to produce such commercials can be well under $1,000. Makes you shake your head in disbelief when you learn that many companies spend as much as $500,000 for commercials that do no more than entertain.

To produce a $1,000 commercial that outperforms the $500,000 variety, remember that you must make your product or service fascinating. People view TV spots with an eye toward what's in it for them. TV is about pictures more than words. People pay attention to TV spots with only a tiny fraction of their mind, so they won't follow complex ideas. Simplicity wins every time.

Your commercial will grab attention if it is funny, dazzling, and full of fancy visuals. If you create such a commercial, however, you take the risk that viewers will remember the wrong things. It's like saying nothing to everybody. Better than saying everything to nobody, I suppose. But guerrillas always opt to say something to somebody. By doing so, they maximize every dollar they invest in television advertising, still the reigning champion of marketing.

86

The adage believed by the vast majority of small business owners is that you get what you pay for. The adage favored by business owners of the guerrilla variety is that you get more than you pay for.

Guerrillas may pay an artist a high price for a single piece of artwork for, say, an ad, getting what they pay for. Then, after disclosing this to the artist, they use the same artwork on a brochure, a circular, a sign. They use it in on a point-of-purchase display, a package, a self-mailer, a TV spot. Certainly they make it an important part of their Web site. And this isn't the end of the value they derive from their original investment: the guerrilla uses the artwork over a period of years, featuring it as a major or minor part of a myriad of marketing weapons, spreading the cost of the investment over time. When you look back on the many uses to which you've put it and the duration of its value, you know you've received much more than you paid for. And if you pay for excellent artwork in the first place, your economic savvy is invisible to everybody but you. You don't appear to be pinching pennies, but you are.

If you know that *you can get extra mileage from many marketing investments,* you can make your investments pay off handsomely for you. Before making the investment, always ask yourself how you'll maximize its benefit to you. If you can't enhance its value by extending its usage, think twice. Are there other marketing investments that can do double or triple the work for you?

Some guerrillas enlarge a single piece of artwork or photograph to poster-size, some to billboard-size. Many transform their ads into signs, their circulars into mailers, their video brochures into TV spots. They may invest in a music track and use it as background music in their TV spots, radio advertising, on-hold marketing messages, and video and audio brochures. By finding multiple uses for many of the components that make up their marketing arsenal, they are economizing across the board and across the years. Truly they understand the nature of an investment.

Perhaps their most important way to economize is not merely to stretch each dollar but to measure its performance. By tracking the effectiveness of all their marketing weapons, they know which to eliminate completely and which to rely upon more heavily. This provides them with the greatest of all marketing economies — making every dollar work.

87

ore than a few owners of small business are quite economy-minded, but they save their money in all the wrong ways. Shaving costs on the quality of paper stock you'll use for stationery is a false economy. Writing your own direct-mail letters when you have no talent at written persuasion is a false economy. Cutting costs just because you can is no way to economize. Using an amateur because you don't want to pay for a pro, even though one is needed, is not a way to save your money.

If you're advertising on, say, radio four weeks a month, it's all right to cut back to three weeks a month. Your campaign will not be diminished. But if you cut back to one week a month, thinking you'll save even more money, you're engaging in a false economy, not giving radio the chance to repeat your message enough to be absorbed. The public is very adept at forgetting all about you.

Guerrillas never try to save money if the economy will undermine their credibility: an inexpensive investment that doesn't pay off is a waste. A $10 ad that doesn't work costs you a lot more than a $1,000 ad that does work. Doing a direct mailing without a follow-up is another mistake: you're kidding yourself if you expect results but are not willing to invest in them. You *must* be willing to test offers, headlines, copy, prices, media, and ad sizes.

One of the most common false economies is cutting back on marketing itself, often just when the marketing is taking hold, which means a probable loss of the investment in awareness that you've made already. Guerrillas protect that investment. To terminate your *marketing investment to save money is like stopping your wristwatch to save time.* Business will go on and people will continue buying, while business owners who walk away from their investment will forfeit their momentum to their competitors. Another common false economy is the notion that you save by being your own spokesperson for your radio or television spots. Maybe you're good enough to be a convincing presenter, but chances are, you're shooting yourself in the foot in an attempt to save a few bucks. Nothing personal.

It can make sense to run the largest ad in the Yellow Pages if it means you will have the best position in the directory. This doesn't sound economical, but it is *less* economical to invest in an ad that few people will see. The priority must always be not on cost-cutting but on getting the best return on your investment in marketing.

88

Exactly how much money should you budget for your marketing? In 1998, the average investment was 4 percent of gross sales. But guerrillas are never interested in being average, especially considering that the average company goes out of business within five years.

Guerrillas create a marketing budget based on percent of projected gross sales, allowing them to operate in the future rather than the past. Then they direct their energies to staying within that budget while making it work harder for them. They accomplish this simply by keeping careful track of the effectiveness of the weapons they employ.

This allows them to delete media from their plan if those media aren't producing profits. It lets them double up on media that are proving to be superstars. They have the insight to *consider their monthly investment in marketing the same as they consider their rent.* They wouldn't dream of skipping a month's rent just because sales are down. And they wouldn't pay double rent in a month when sales are up.

To stay within your budget, you must turn a deaf ear to the golden-tongued sales representatives from the media who urge you to use their publications, their stations. Their recommendations are sometimes valid. But because you are committed to a marketing plan, you should not buy anything on impulse. Through careful tracking, you may find a way to eliminate some of the media you are presently using and replace them with what the rep is hawking. But don't buy it at the expense of your budget.

Few business owners are happy because they've increased or decreased their budget, but many guerrillas are grinning because they've maintained their budget and beefed up their profits. They've embarked on a series of fusion marketing programs that let them market to more people more frequently without impacting their budget. Online, they abide by the rule of thirds, investing one-third of their online budget in designing and posting their site, one-third in attracting people to it, and one-third in maintaining and improving their site.

When you select a budget to cover your marketing, including your advertising and direct response costs, your Web site and creative costs, figure on investing about 10 percent of that budget in the production of your marketing materials. This is no place to skimp. Be sure you foresee production costs when drafting your budget. As generating profits through marketing should be one of your goals, doing this while staying within your budget should be another.

89

The area of purchasing media is one in which substantial economies may be enjoyed. However, business owners rarely cash in on these economies when they purchase media by themselves. They know media selection is not a do-it-yourself task, so they gladly hand the responsibility off to a media-buying service — a company that does nothing but evaluate, purchase, and negotiate the price of media. Because professional media buyers purchase so much media, they have serious clout at each medium. For example, when you ask them to buy television time for you because you are going to invest $10,000 in the medium, they have the influence of $10 million in television advertising time buys because of their other clients. No wonder they can negotiate a far lower price than you could. The savings they achieve in their purchases ordinarily covers their own modest fees. Because media-buying services are granted a 15 percent discount on radio, television, and magazine purchases (the same as advertising agencies), most keep 5 percent for themselves and present you with a 10 percent discount along with their media-selecting expertise and negotiating skills.

When the media offers time or space for sale, it's like offering smoke for sale. If you don't buy it and nobody else buys it, the time and space disappear and become worthless to the media. Therefore, they are often willing to cut prices for an advertiser. *Never pay what they ask on their rate cards.*

Media-buying services can not only save you vast sums of money, but also offer sage counsel on which media to purchase, whether you can afford to run full-color ads rather than black-and-white ads, which publications offer regional editions, what days are best to run ads, which times are best to run radio and TV spots, which TV channels makes most sense, which radio stations will be the most cooperative. They will alert you that the cost per thousand exposures to your message is not as important as the cost per prospect.

The world of media is complex and dangerous for beginners. Enter it at your own risk — or connect with an experienced guide in the form of a company that knows media backward and forward. You sure don't want to say the right thing in the right way to the wrong people. Professional media buyers can help you stay on course with your marketing, while saving you so much money that you feel you're getting more than you're paying for.

Media rate cards for both print and electronic media are akin to works of fiction — fascinating to read but without a basis in truth. Guerrillas pride themselves on paying less but getting more from the media they employ.

90

Because their marketing budgets are usually small, guerrillas do all they can to maximize the results of every dollar spent. Connect your advertising campaigns with your Web sites and PR campaigns, in-store displays, and trade show booths. You must have a cohesive marketing plan: each weapon pulls in the same direction and communicates the same message, giving you the benefit of synergy.

Make copies of your ads and post them wherever possible, include them in mailings, and post them on your Web site. Do not advertise unless you *know* it is best for your marketing plan. Advertising is simply *one* component of a marketing plan.

Guerrillas have the insight that *the better their staff knows their marketing, the more effectively it will pay off.* Therefore, keep all of your employees — from your sales force to the people answering telephones — abreast of all the marketing activities. Use all of your marketing materials to sell something in addition to the planned purchase. Your package helps to enlarge the size of the transaction by featuring a special offer. Same for their invoices, receipts, direct-response coupons, anything that their customers see.

Instead of mass mailings, think of personal mailings. Try, for instance, to send twenty-five personal letters each week. Not a big cost, but definitely a big payoff. Keep your mailing lists *updated*

— 10 percent of the names go out of the market each year. When a prospect responds to one of your marketing efforts, do all you can to close the sale, because 66 percent of the responders will eventually make a purchase within the year — either from you or from a competitor.

Guerrillas foresee difficulties and unresolved problems that might arise, then contend with them before they detract from their marketing. They are never price-obsessed as indicated by their refusal to rely on constant discount sales and their willingness to pay more if it means a better value.

To get the most from a tiny budget, consider marketing to a smaller niche, such as the bank that targeted only the wealthiest one-half of one percent of the population. Embrace a cause — 90 percent of consumers are likely to respond to it even if it means paying a higher price.

Alas, guerrillas know well the rule of twice: it will probably cost you twice what you think it will to remain truly competitive online as technologies advance and evolve. What can you do about this horrible fact? *Plan for it,* so that you can stay competitive.

CHAPTER ELEVEN

INSIGHTS INTO ATTACKING

91

To fulfill a guerrilla's dreams, a guerrilla marketing attack must have ten components. Nine aren't enough. The astute small business owner begins assembling these components from the future before starting in the present. First, envision a goal — have a clear vision of what you will accomplish three years down the road, and five, and ten. This goal must be *crystal clear* — you must see it down to the last detail. The more clearly you envision your plan, the better prepared you are to start out the right way.

Second, the guerrilla crafts a plan, a simple seven-sentence plan. Its structure is laid out in Chapter 2. The attack is quite simple so far — have a goal and know how you plan to achieve it. The third component is a leader, probably the person who envisioned the goal and crafted the plan, but it may be someone better qualified to lead the journey to the goal.

The fourth component, which moves the attack from paper and into the real world, is a time to commit, a specific date that will mark the launching of your first weapon. Make it a realistic date so that you don't start attacking from behind the start line and have to move at double time to catch up to your plan.

The fifth component is an arsenal of weapons that you select as ideal to help you reach your target audience in the most effective manner. Each weapon should move you closer to your goal. The sixth component is insight to market with the acumen of a guerrilla. Reading this book indicates that you already possess this weapon. The seventh component is insight as well, this time courtesy of your own research — *insight into your competition and your audience.*

It sounds as though you should be ready to roll, but you're not there yet. The eighth component is a system that will provide constant reconnaissance over your attack to detect which weapons are producing and which are draining profits. Plan for that at the start or you begin wasting money from the start.

The ninth component is fortitude. Problems will arise, unforeseen circumstances will pop up in your face, Murphy will rear his ugly head to zap both your technology and your psyche, competitors will play dirty, and frustration will wait around every corner. You will be able to address such problems because you have the farsightedness to know they're coming and the fortitude to attack them. The tenth component begins your march to your goal — it's knowing exactly what step to take next. That's why the next insight illuminates that step, along with the steps that follow.

92

To master guerrilla marketing, you must stockpile the components necessary to hit the jackpot. You need to do the right things at the right time, never moving into terrain that hasn't been reconnoitered. The mastery process calls for astute knowledge of who your ideal customers will be and companion knowledge about what your competitors are doing to win the hearts of those people. Know the specific reasons why your potential customers should be attracted to your business — this is all crucial information that you must gather before you even draft your marketing strategy.

The insight for you to take to the bank is that *the first step of your attack is the gaining of knowledge.* Through intensive research you must learn of your potential market and how they're being wooed currently; then you can address the best ways to influence these people. No attack can succeed if you're oblivious to details concerning your prospects and competitors.

Only after taking that first step are you ready for the second step — committing to writing the benefits you offer, the competitive advantages that will turn your business into a magnet for prospects, the services you offer that make you stand apart, the details of your excellence. The third step is the selection of marketing weapons you'll use to make your attack lethal and cost-effective.

Your research will have informed you as to which weapons are most appropriate to reach your target market.

Now, it's time for the fourth step — drafting your seven-sentence guerrilla marketing plan. Now you know what to say in it. The fifth step is to put everything together in a calendar that dictates the weapons and the timing, listing the specific media you'll use and the monthly costs involved. The calendar is a promise you're making to yourself. The sixth step is to locate and team up with your fusion marketing partners. You'll find many who are eager to tie in with your guerrilla efforts.

Step seven is where the action begins — pulling the trigger and firing the first rounds of marketing directly at your audience. This is the launch of your attack — weapon by weapon, orderly yet unpredictable. The eighth step is one of the toughest, the step on which most business owners stumble: maintaining the attack. Maintaining the attack is the real meat and potatoes of guerrilla marketing. The ninth step is assessing the results of your efforts, evaluating each weapon with an eye toward discontinuing the ones that didn't cover their act and augmenting those that did.

This step naturally leads to the tenth step, an ongoing process of improving your attack in every detail. Only by taking all ten steps in the right order do you master the art of guerrilla marketing.

93

An insight for you to embrace is that *a guerrilla marketing attack is never-ending.* It has a beginning, a middle, but never an end, for it is a process. You improve it, perfect it, change it, even pause in it. But you never stop it completely.

Of all ten steps in succeeding with a guerrilla marketing attack, steps eight, nine, and ten take the most time. You spend a relatively brief time developing the attack and inaugurating it, but you spend the life of your business maintaining, monitoring, and improving your attack. At no point should you take anything for granted. At no point should you fall into the pit of self-satisfaction because your attack is working. Never forget that others, very smart and motivated competitors, are studying you and doing their utmost to surpass you in the marketing arena.

Guerrillas thrive and prosper because they understand the deeper meanings of the phrases "customer base" and "long-term commitment." This enables them to reinvent their marketing — just as long as they are firm in their commitment to their existing customers and prospects. An attack without flexibility is in danger of failing. But that flexibility does not allow you to take your eyes off the needs of your customers.

Keep alert for new niches at which you can aim your attack. Large companies don't have the luxury of profiting from a narrow niche. No matter how successful your attack, never lose contact with your customers. If you do, you lose your competitive advantage over huge companies that have too many layers of bureaucracy for personal contact. Guerrilla marketing is authentic; it never acts or feels impersonal. It never feels like selling.

Philip Kotler, the author of *Marketing Management,* says, "Authentic marketing is not the art of selling what you make but knowing what to make. It is the art of identifying and understanding customer needs and creating solutions that deliver satisfaction to the customers, profits to the producers, and benefits for the stakeholders. Market innovation is gained by creating customer satisfaction through product innovation, product quality, and customer service. It these are absent, no amount of advertising, sales promotion, or salesmanship can compensate."

Your attack must be characterized by a strong tie with your own target audience. You know them. You serve them. They know it. Guerrilla attacks do not suffer from your lack of resources, but instead prosper because lack of capital makes them more willing to try new and innovative ideas, concepts ripe for guerrillas but not for huge companies.

94

Your attack will succeed in direct relationship to how focused you are. Guerrillas have the insight that *precision strengthens an attack.* They know the enormous difference between their prospects and their prime prospects. They are aware of the gigantic chasm separating their customers from their best customers. This perspective enables them to narrow their aim at the best prospects that marketing money can buy and the finest customers ever to grace their customer list.

They are fully cognizant that it doesn't take much more work to sell a subscription to a magazine than to sell a single issue. That's why their marketing attack is devoted to motivating people to subscribe to their businesses psychologically.

Once you have a customer, do all you can to intensify the relationship; do not treat all customers and prospects equally. Consider the menswear chain with a database of 47,000 names. Mailings never involve more than 3,000 pieces at a time. Who receives the mail? Says the owner, "Only the people appropriate to mail to." When he received trousers of a specific style, he mailed information about them only to those customers to whom he was certain they'd appeal — and enjoyed a 30 percent response rate.

The cost of his mailing was a tiny fraction of the size of his profits. There's not a chance of reveling in such a healthy response unless you're targeting your mailing with absolute precision. It's a necessity in a world where postal charges and paper prices are both slated to increase. Unless you're hitting the bull's-eye, you're wasting your marketing investment.

Your attack should focus on helping. You have to market selectively and comprehensively. Think not in terms of selling or befriending as much as helping. This means zeroing in on your best prospects and staying with them once they've been identified as prime. Will it take three approaches to win them over? Or will it take three years? Both answers will win out over those who think they can mail to less-than-prime customers only one time, those who use scattershot, broad-based, imprecise marketing plans.

The benefit of precision is that it allows you to get personal. Recall the nonprofit organization that increased its response rate by 668 percent by paying special attention to its big donors — sending them a handwritten envelope using a commemorative stamp and a handwritten twenty-five-word note at the end of the letter. The cost to do this was low indeed, and the payoff proved the value of precision and focus in a guerrilla marketing attack.

95

Once you've launched your own guerrilla marketing attack, everything well in place and proceeding according to your plan, you've got to be armed with realistic expectations. Hoping for the impossible or unlikely can undo all your good efforts and render your attack ineffective, not to mention frustrating.

Realistic expectations mean facing up to the fact that the vast majority of people haven't a clue about your business, don't know what you stand for, how you can help them, and why they should pay any attention to you in the first place. This means that most of your target market is apathetic to you and begins to know about you from a standing start.

Guerrillas are buoyed by the insight that *even the best marketing doesn't take effect immediately.* Although you must curry the favor of your existing customer base, you need to reach out to the enormous number of potential customers who don't yet know of your quality and service. And this can't happen overnight.

A well-crafted guerrilla marketing attack may not make itself known to your cash flow until three months after you've launched it. And then, only a glimmer of its effectiveness reveals itself to you. Six months after launch, you should have a solid feeling that your marketing is working for you in the ways you hoped it would work.

Your marketing is analogous to the pounding of a nail through a hardwood board. You'd never expect the first tap of the hammer to do the job. You'd never expect to hammer the nail through that board with even the first five blows of your hammer. To succeed is to take many raps of the hammer, but you must stay with the one hole you started. Making changes in your marketing shortly after you've put it into action is like starting a new hole each time you drop the hammer; do so, and you'll never get through to the other side that way.

Changing your strategy is akin to looking for a soft spot on the hardboard. It's not there. Don't expect it to be. You can sharpen your nail with a better message, but take your mind off of soft spots and stay with the spot you started — using a sharper nail.

Word-of-mouth marketing can help you unless you rely upon it too much. It's silly to expect customers to do all the heavy lifting for you. But you'll gain word-of-mouth momentum if you increase your awareness and visibility with a perpetual attack. I'm not asking you to lower your expectations, just to expect them at a realistic time.

96

E very attack needs a commander, and I suggest that the commander of your attack be you. Yes, I know that a designated guerrilla might be able to handle the task for you because you're so involved in finances or selling, in management or production, but the reality is that the best CEOs never delegate the marketing function. The insight possessed by the guerrilla is manifested in *the guerrilla's involvement in the marketing process: he or she must be part of it.* Your marketing department should be *lean.* Guerrillas are big on delegating, but marketing is not one of the things they delegate. If you delegate, you are too removed from the customer. Customer proximity is *crucial* for the guerrilla. Customer contact is essential. You never hear of companies losing clients because of too much contact, but you do hear horror tales of being dropped due to lack of contact.

The more personal contact you have with customers, the less you'll have to rely on market research, which is too often used as a master rather than a guide, and an impersonal one at that. Research is used as a supplement, but never a substitute for face-to-face consumer understanding.

To maintain a guerrilla marketing attack, develop personal relationships with your best customers while learning the most you can about them. Track every lead you get, every phone call, every

Web site you visit — but at the same time, learn to respect your customers as individuals. They must never be perceived as statistics. In almost every small business success, a small group of individuals is at the core of the business. This is true even of large businesses. For example, a business that sells one yogurt brand to 100 million households learned that a mere 1 million of those households contribute to more than 50 percent of the total profit.

Guerrillas aim their marketing plan not at large segments of people, but at a core group of loyal customers. They don't define their market in terms of demographics, such as housewives aged 28–42 with two children living at home, but in terms of behavior, habits, and needs, such as dog lovers or business-opportunity seekers, as golfers or gourmet cooks. Then you can develop new products and services targeted to the audience you know so well. The Grateful Dead, one of the most successful marketing organizations in America, sells not just live entertainment, but CDs, clothes, and food. Old-fashioned marketing called for loyalty to a product category and the pursuit of new customers. Today, guerrilla marketing calls for loyalty to a customer group and the development of new offerings for that group.

97

Guerrillas know well that 80 percent of their business comes from 20 percent of their products or services and that 20 percent of their customers help generate 80 percent of their profits. Not only are they able to identify the less productive 80 percent and the very effective 20 percent, but they have the insight to *do something about it* — eliminating some offerings, heavily promoting others, paying attention to everyone on their mailing list, and paying special attention to the favored 20 percent.

The 80–20 rule applies with shining clarity to marketing. The only way for you to know which component of your marketing is the most effective is to measure the results of everything you do. This crucial part of marketing is called quantification. Innovations and new weapons are important, but you must quantify them to be certain they're producing the desired results.

Once you've learned which marketing efforts work best for you, it's time for the process known as orchestration. Says entrepreneurial expert Michael Gerber, "Orchestration is the elimination of discretion or choice at the operating level of your business." Once you've determined the best methods of marketing, standardize the process as much as possible. Customers want *consistency*.

McDonald's starts with the same kind of potato at each franchise. Each potato is then cut into exactly the same size pieces, cooked in the same kind of oil in the same kind of fryer at the same temperature for exactly the same amount of time. Once you determine the marketing that works best for you, consistency will make it work even harder for you. Standardization will be your friend.

You and your staff must never forget to ask the crucial question: How did you hear about us? Meticulously keep track of the answers, because those answers are going to point to your best method of marketing. Your customers actually keep track for you, but you must ask them that crucial question. And then you have to act on what you've learned.

Make your employees, the people who answer your telephone, everyone who comes into contact with prospects, aware of exactly how important it is to track your marketing. A depressingly large 80 percent of your investment in it will be wasted, and if you don't know which 80 percent, you are in very serious trouble and surely not a guerrilla.

Two-thirds of all marketing expenditures are now invested in direct marketing such as direct mail, telemarketing, Web marketing, and infomercials because they are all *accountable*. They let you keep track.

98

As Aristotle reminds us that excellence isn't a goal but a process, Levinson reminds you that a guerrilla marketing attack is a sham unless it continues to improve from the day you launch it. Improving the profitability of your attack is the reason for tracking it. Guerrillas have the insight to realize *there are many areas in which improvement is possible.*

They begin by trying to improve the quality of the product or service they offer. They monitor this area with customer research shortly after the sale. Questionnaires help them find areas where they fall short of perfection, pointing the way to where they should improve.

You can almost always rework and upgrade your selection of media. Each medium you use should be scrutinized with the goal of eliminating the ones that aren't doing the job for you. By the end of the year, you should have a good fix on which are booms and which are busts. Your Web site, as a living marketing weapon, must be improved every week it's online. You must also improve the response rates from the lists of people to whom you are directing your marketing. It's estimated that 60 percent of your success depends on the right media, 30 percent on the right offer, and 10 percent on the creativity of the presentation.

Your message must constantly be improved by tracking responses to your offers. Create a benchmark response rate, then measure all other response rates against it. Rather than major overhauls, tweaking often does the job. Improve your profitability by experimenting with different prices. Lowering or raising those prices can have a positive impact on your profits, but you won't know the right price until you've tested several. Remember that you're not trying to improve your sales, only your profits.

The attitude of your employees can be improved as you go along, getting them to tune in to your wavelength, be energized by your passion, and share your vision. Employee training is the way to accomplish this. Some experts believe that $1 invested in communicating with your staff is worth $10 communicating with the trade, and $100 spent talking to customers.

As your attack continues, consistently improve your systems for measuring media, message, employees, customer satisfaction — systems used to gain referrals, data, new fusion marketing partners. Guerrillas improve their follow-up, both in the number of contacts and the quality of follow-up. If it results in more repeat business and referrals, it's working. If not, improve it. Winston Churchill said, "To improve is to change; to be perfect is to change often." Improving is as much a process as is marketing.

99

A guerrilla marketing attack usually entails the presenting of a proposal. It's at proposal time that the rubber meets the road. If you present anything but a guerrilla proposal, it means that all the marketing you've done up till that time has probably been wasted. Sheer agony. Guerrillas employ specific tactics to make sure that their courtship activities lead to a long-term business marriage. Qualify your prospects so that the marriage doesn't die during the honeymoon. Never walk into a prospect's office as a complete stranger — you must *forge a bond before you make the proposal.*

Guerrillas identify a real need that their prospects have and know they can fill that need better than anyone else. They are absolutely certain that the prospect to whom they are making their proposal can use their products or services right now and not at some future date. They present their proposals only to people who are the ultimate decision-makers and can give them the go-ahead immediately without having to check with higher authorities. Guerrillas rehearse their presentation till they've got it down pat. They decide ahead of time exactly what they want to show and tell, then play back their chosen words with graphics, and always ask for the order at the conclusion of the proposal.

Prepare a document to leave with your prospects after the proposal has been presented. The document summarizes the high points of the proposal, is completely self-contained, and includes important facts and figures that might have bogged down the actual presentation. Design your proposals to address your prospect's goals clearly. Do this with a single sentence that proves you are oriented to those goals. Find ways to repeat that sentence several times during the presentation of your proposal, Guerrillas present their proposals in a logical manner so that one point flows naturally to the next, making the proposal very simple to follow. They know that the organization of their proposal is nearly as important as the content. They talk about the prospect's business and not about their own.

When making a proposal, you must make the prospect like you, like your company, and love what your company can do for them. Because guerrillas are keen about follow-up, they follow-up their proposals with a thank-you note within twenty-four hours of the presentation. The follow-up is directed to the person who has the authority to say yes, and has as a goal the setting of a start date. Your greatest allies in a guerrilla proposal are your knowledge of the prospect, your enthusiasm during the presentation, and the personal bonding you have already established.

100

N ow that you're ready to mount your attack, take a moment to consider the state of business around the world right at this moment. A lot has changed, and guerrillas have the insight to *keep abreast of the changes.*

Actual matter matters less than ever. Processing information is astonishingly more powerful and cost-effective than moving physical products. The value of a company is found these days not in tangible assets, but in people, ideas, and key information-driven assets.

Distance seems to have vanished. The world is now your customer. And your competitor. Geography used to be the name of the game, but the Internet has changed that forever — giving you more opportunities around the globe, and more competitors at the same time.

Time has collapsed. That means instant interactivity is critical. In an era when time is more important than money, there's a premium on instant response and the ability to adapt to your marketplace in real time. Winning companies embrace constant improvement and offer time savings.

People are more important than ever and they know it. Enormous value comes from smart ideas, along with the business systems they create. Every successful technology was conceived of by a bright human being.

The Internet can dramatically boost the adoption of a product or service by network-enhanced word-of-mouth marketing. Communication is now so easy that product awareness spreads like wildfire. Being first out of the block has never been more important.

Buyers have gained power and sellers have gained opportunity. Your competitors are only a mouse click away as people learn that they are what they click. The meaning: you must offer unique services or lower costs.

Marketing is transforming into a one-on-one activity. Information is much easier to customize than hard goods, so the information portion of any product or service is becoming a larger part of its total value. Custom tailoring and custom marketing rules.

Every product is available everywhere. The gap between desire and purchase has closed. Instead of remembering, merely clicking on the "buy" button is enough. This merges marketing with fulfillment. The Internet knows no bounds and people can now easily act on impulses. Guerrillas are aware of these changes, adjust their marketing and expectations accordingly, and realize that more changes are sure to come. Many can be used to add firepower to a guerrilla marketing attack.

CHAPTER TWELVE

INSIGHTS INTO ACTION

The karate master learns everything necessary to slam his hand through the wooden board. He doesn't even think about the board, only about seeing his hand on the other side of it. The shattering of the board is not part of his vision. The board is merely an illusion to him, and his hand beneath the cracked board is the only reality the karate master will accept. Theory is what helped him earn his black belt, but he never would have earned it if he had not taken action. Obstacles that he encountered on his way to mastery were merely illusions. All the successes he achieved were reality. As a master, he is aware of the illusion but focused upon the reality. And he realizes that his insights into karate and energy, into force and concentration, are the power behind his action. *Insight plus action equals success.*

To master guerrilla marketing is to take action. You cannot merely read a book and absorb the insights. The mastery of guerrilla marketing has *action* at its very core. Without action, there can be no mastery. Without action, there exists only the illusion of mastery, but never the results, never the fruits of having mastered what others only flail at.

Guerrillas understand that there are two realities in life: The major one is illusion, the minor one is reality. The better connected the two are in your own life, the wiser you are, the better primed for success.

A key to mastery is to recognize each reality for what it is. To buy into illusion and mistake it for reality is to delude yourself. That delusion is no illusion. Now that you have the insights to master guerrilla marketing, you can convert the illusion of mastering it into reality. Do this by taking concrete action.

Guerrillas know they can change reality just as they can change illusion. To most people on earth, *illusion is reality.* Shall I repeat that because it is so pivotal to your understanding? Because so few people understand it? Then I will: to the majority of earth's citizens, illusion is reality. In fact, to them, it's the only reality. Yet guerrillas who have mastered marketing are blessed with the perception to know illusion from reality and the wisdom to control both. Unless there is action, there can be no control. Ask the karate master.

Both karate master and guerrilla will tell you that karate and marketing exist first as a state of mind. Guerrilla marketing begins with a clear view of the end, the goals towards which guerrilla strive. Their minds upon those goals, the rest of their actions are foretold by the clarity of their focus on that goal.

Although guerrillas are famed for their patience, they never wait too long. Harking back to General George Patton's words, "A good plan implemented today is better than a perfect plan implemented tomorrow." Perfection is merely the object of your quest and not something you will attain — at least not for very long. Rather than beginning with perfection, perfect your activities *as you attack.*

Metamorphosing yourself into a guerrilla may seem to be a daunting task, but it really isn't. Mastering guerrilla marketing isn't something that you do overnight, though the decision to do so happens in a flashing instant. The mastery of marketing is something so seemingly complex that you may not be sure where to start. Chapter 11 gave you steps to follow, each one in order, but even the thought of taking these steps sets some business owners back on their heels. Not to worry. Your task can easily be broken down into several small parts, each one simple enough for you to handle gracefully. Divide big tasks into smaller tasks. Never underestimate the power of your own gut reaction. Your most valuable aid in hitting pay dirt with guerrilla marketing is your ability to *prioritize* the actions you must take.

You also need to be able to dream, then to breathe life into those dreams. Henry David Thoreau said, "If you have built castles in the air, your work need not be lost; that is where they should be. Now, put the foundations under them."

The foundations begin with words. Guerrillas know well the enormous power of written words. The ancient Egyptians thought that words were magic. They believed that if you write it, surely it will happen. That's why a guerrilla marketing attack, a guerrilla marketing mindset, begins with a plan that is put into words. Success is not something that will happen to you. It will flow through you — to your staff, your customers, to future generations, and to the body of knowledge that comprises our small business wisdom of today. The flow begins when you write those first words. Not a lot of words — a mere seven sentences will contain all the words you need to begin. Those sentences are your first steps in the endless marathon. They will keep you on the right course.

When you're on that course, your marketing will be indistinguishable from the rest of your company. Everything about your business will carry the messages of quality and service, of conscientiousness and caring. Your product or service, your staff and yourself, your attitude and reputation, will be part of your marketing and your marketing part of them. And it all will begin with you putting words on paper — or on screen.

Can marketing really be that simple — putting a course of action into writing and then taking that action on a consistent basis? That's it. That's how simple marketing can be. It's not a secret. It's not a formula. It's also not easy and not instant.

Many business owners realize the simplicity of marketing, but don't know where to begin. Analysis paralysis stops them in their tracks. So many tasks. Where to start? They know what they must do, but don't have a plan, so they make disconnected efforts to achieve a hazy goal. When they don't see immediate results, they lose confidence, if any existed in the first place.

If there's a correct time to start, it's right now. If there's a proper place, it's right where you are. You'll never feel that you are completely ready, so you may as well begin right now.

This is the secret: take action and never stop. You heard Diana Ross sing when she was a member of the Supremes. This is what she said about taking action: "You can't just sit there and wait for people to give you that golden dream; you've got to get out there and make it happen for yourself." The best time to market is when you don't need more business. The best source of new clients is old clients, and the most successful marketing plan is characterized by quality, not quantity. Your best marketing vehicle, and least expensive, is a satisfied customer. And the two best ways to measure your marketing are by customer retention and profits, which are contingent on each other.

Look at your marketing plan the same as you look at your rent: you pay it and never think twice. Marketing is also analogous to breathing: you couldn't exist with only one breath, or even two or three. Don't think you're going to attract a new customer with only one effort, or even two or three. You keep breathing and stay alive. You keep marketing and stay profitable.

Every part of your success is dependent upon one individual. You are that individual. You're in charge. You say when to begin. You have the insight to make the right decisions now. To succeed, you're going to need that insight, along with courage and conscientiousness. If you're frightened of making mistakes, you're sunk. Accept the fact that you'll make mistakes. Each mistake will teach you a lesson.

Michael Eisner, chairman and CEO of Disney, says, "At a certain level, what we do at Disney is very simple. We set our goals, aim for perfection, inevitably fall short, try to learn from our mistakes, and hope that our successes will continue to outnumber our failures." There's nothing Mickey Mouse about that kind of philosophy, for it embraces mistakes as part of the process.

There is no need to hit a home run the first time you're at bat. A single will do, then another single, then another, one following the other — none grandiose, but each bringing you closer to your goal.

All along, it is essential that you know the answers to the seven questions posed by Louis Patler in his book *Don't Compete . . . Tilt the Field!*

- What business are you in?
- What other businesses are you in?
- What are you core competencies?
- What are you core values?
- Which competitor will be your next partner?
- Are your short-term goals and long-term strategies aligned?
- Do your answers to the above questions complement one another?

These questions don't have simple answers, but these are the questions you must ask and answer to have confidence you're heading in the right direction and have all that you need to reach your destination.

As small business grows, so does the need for mastering guerrilla marketing. And small business is growing faster than ever. As entrepreneurs arise all over the globe, so does the need to master guerrilla marketing. Simply a new kid on the block as the twentieth century headed toward its completion, guerrilla marketing is now a powerful and proven force worldwide. It must be reckoned with and, best yet, utilized. Some would say it's mandatory for small business survival. Ask any small business owner — it's far easier to employ guerrilla marketing than hope to defend yourself against it.

A whale of a lot has changed since I wrote the first guerrilla marketing book in 1984. And almost all of the change favors small business. Marketing itself has changed dramatically and interactively, not to mention electronically. So has the array of weapons available to guerrillas — more powerful than ever, yet half of them completely free. That's why so many guerrillas are smiling so broadly. They also know that many things have not changed and that those things are as important as the things that have.

I'm referring to the soul and essence of guerrilla marketing, which remain, as always, achieving conventional goals, such as profits and joy, with unconventional methods, such as investing energy instead of money. I'm also referring to humanity, which is relatively unchanged since the first book, indeed, since the first human.

It's not possible to ignore the fact that we're in a new century. If you look into the hearts and minds of your prospects, you'll see that very little has changed there, too. Certainly there's a growing awareness of the precious and elusive nature of time, perhaps even a bit more humanity, made possible by, of all things, technology.

The marketing world has changed because it has shrunk rather than expanded. Again, credit technology for the shrink job, accomplished not as much by the jet as the net. Marketing has also become a lot more technical. But that doesn't mean you have to be technical — because technology has met you more than halfway by becoming much easier to use and even easier to pay for.

Guerrillas welcome the changes as much as they welcome the status quos. They are fully alert to what has changed and what must never change. They know well the difference between change and improvement.

Guerrilla Marketing started out a single volume and has since acted biblically by being fruitful and multiplying into a library of eighteen books and counting, a CD-ROM, an abundance of video and audiotapes, a newsletter, a valuable Web site at www.gmarket-ing.com, an internationally syndicated column for newspapers, magazines, and the Internet, and presentations and speaking in enough countries for us to consider forming our own Guerrilla United Nations.

But that wouldn't be very conducive to the guerrilla's natural advantages of being lean, flexible, and fast on his feet. That would be opting for largeness, which might get in the way of the warmth and closeness for which guerrillas strive. That would be the expected in a world where guerrillas are famed for doing the unexpected.

The need for guerrilla marketing can be seen in the light of three facts.

1. Because of big business downsizing, decentralization, relaxation of government regulations, affordable technology, and a revolution in consciousness, people around the world are gravitating to small business in record numbers.
2. Small business failures are also establishing record numbers and one of the main reasons for the failures is a failure to understand marketing.
3. Guerrilla marketing has been proven in action to work for small businesses around the world. It works because it's simple to understand, easy to implement, and outrageously inexpensive.

Guerrilla marketing is needed because it gives small businesses a delightfully unfair advantage: certainty in an uncertain world, economy in a high-priced world, simplicity in a complicated world, marketing awareness in a clueless world.

Is marketing really going to be all that different in the twenty-first century? The answers are no and yes. Although the core of marketing will remain making a powerful offer to the right people, the ways and means of making that offer now vary dramatically as the Internet emerges from its infancy and begins toddling — in any direction you want if you're a guerrilla. And the people who whom the offers are being made are far more sophisticated and enlightened than ever. If there's anything a guerrilla likes, it's a well-informed prospect.

The need for guerrilla marketing these days is about equal to the need for a steering wheel on a car that will speed faster than ever on roads that twist more than ever, actually changing direction as you drive upon them! Scary, huh? Not scary for guerrillas who operate with both wheels and wings. Not scary for guerrillas who know the terrain.

This book has presented you with a clear map of the terrain. It has provided you with a vehicle to navigate the terrain with stability and grace and the savvy to use it with skill. Most importantly, this book gives both of us the answer to an important question.

I hear the question after I give a guerrilla marketing talk. I hear the question after I host a guerrilla marketing online conference. I hear the question after I complete a marketing consultation with a client.

The question is: "Is everything you're saying about guerrilla marketing between the covers of a single book?"

The answer is: "It is now."

Because it is, you are ready to master guerrilla marketing now. You now have the insights to master guerrilla marketing and make its tactics your avenues to profits that surpass your most ambitious goals.

The mastery of guerrilla marketing provides your illumination and your power. Use it wisely. Use it aggressively.

INDEX

Patler, Louis, 239
Patton, George (General), 236
PDAs (personal digital assistants), viii
Pepsi, 6
Personality flaws, 139–40
Plan, marketing. *See* Marketing plan
Planning. *See also* Marketing plan
  action in, 21–22
  goal statement in, 17–18
  how to, 13–14
  research before, 15–16
Prioritization, 237
Product, 15, 23, 38, 117–18
Promotion, 84, 85–86, 93–94, 174
Proposals, 117–18, 229–30
Prospects
  and brochures, 45–46
  courtship with, 129–30
  and databases, 181–82
  description of, 127
  as direct marketing focus, 104, 105
  effects of advertising on, 54
  effects of credibility on, 163–64
  and 80–20 rule, 226
  free consultations for, 43–44
  getting attention of, 7–8, 115–16, 173–74
  and marketing attack, 219
  networking with, 161–62
  and planning, 16
  proposals to, 117–18, 229–30
  and timing, 151–52
  using catalogs to reach, 113–14
  using classified ads to reach, 59–60
  using magazines to reach, 75
  using signs to reach, 65
  using TV to reach, 61
  using Yellow Pages to reach, 71–72
PRWEB, 93
Psychology, marketing, 135–36
Public relations (PR), 73–74, 93, 198, 209
Purchase decision, 152

Questionnaires, 56

Radio advertising
  bartering for, 73
  cost of, 64
  cost of, *versus* brochures, 45
  as direct-response method, 111–12
  and economizing, 202, 207–8
  establishing familiarity with, 119–20
  and false economy, 203
  and free consultations, 43–44
  lack of profitability in, 7
  power of, 77
  as show host, 48
  types of, 63–64
  using jingles in, 64
  using PR for, 74
Reconnaissance system, 214
Referral program, 9, 49–50, 53–54
Rejection, 68
Repetition
  and cross-promotion, 70
  difficulty of achieving, 73
  importance of, 64
  and online marketing, 89–90
  power of, 195–96
  in proposals, 230
Reprints, 47, 76
Research
  for direct-response marketing, 121–22

and use with other media, 69–70
using PR to get, 74
Ten guerrilla character traits, 125–
26
Thoreau, Henry David, 237
Time (magazine), 76, 121–22
Timing, 151–52
Tomlinson, Ray, 183
Trust, customer, 135–36
Twain, Mark, 183

Uniqueness
attitude of, 165–66
and competitive advantage, 38
in direct-response marketing,
115–16
in Yellow Pages advertising, 72

Videotapes, 42, 45–46, 202
Virtual, 171. *See also* Technology
VirtualPROMOTE, 93
Visibility, 89–90

Weapons
advertising as, 53–54
brochures as, 45–46
competitive advantage as, 37–38
expertise as, 47–48
follow-up as, 55–56
free consultations as, 43–44
fusion marketing as, 51–52
generosity as, 41–42
Internet as (*See* Internet marketing; Online marketing; Technology; Web site marketing)
for marketing attack, 213–14,
215–16, 240

and marketing plan, 10, 24
PDAs (personal digital assistants) as, viii
referral program as, 49–50
selection of, 179–80
Web site marketing. *See also* Internet marketing; Online marketing
content of, 91–92
and creativity, 7
and credibility, 164
and cross-promotion, 209
and customer relationships, 137,
224
and economizing, 196
and fusion marketing, 52, 198
and improvement, 227
inclusion in budget of, 206
promotion of, 84, 85–86, 93–94
and research, 185–86
uses of, 173–74
and use with other media, 69–70
visibility of, 89–90
World Wide Web, ix. *See also* Online marketing

Yellow Pages advertising
and credibility, 164
and economizing, 204
as marketing medium, 71–72
power of, 78
and relation to marketing, 32
and use with other media, 69–70

Zen Buddhism, 151

Continue your guerrilla mastery
with *The Guerrilla Marketing Newsletter* . . .

Published continuously since 1986, *The Guerrilla Marketing Newsletter* provides you with state-of-the-moment insights to maximize the profits you can obtain through marketing — both online and offline. The newsletter furnishes you with the latest cream of the new guerrilla marketing information from around the world, along with new perspectives on existing wisdom about marketing. It's filled with practical advice, the latest research, upcoming trends, brand-new and valuable marketing techniques — all designed to pay off in handsome profits to you.

A yearly subscription costs $59 for six issues.

All subscribers are given this unique guarantee: If you aren't convinced after examining your first issue for 30 days that the newsletter will raise your profits, your subscription fee will be refunded — along with $2 just for trying.

To subscribe, call, write, fax, or e-mail us at:

> Guerrilla Marketing International
> 260 Cascade Drive, P.O. Box 1336
> Mill Valley, CA 94902, U.S.A.
> 1-800-748-6444
> Fax: 415-381-8361
> E-mail: GMINTL@aol.com

If you're online, visit the Guerrilla Marketing Online Web site. It's the largest small-business marketing Web site on the Internet and makes many offers that are just too generous to miss. Example: You can sign up to receive a daily Guerrilla Marketing Communique online for only $2 per year! Find our Web site at www.gmarketing.com.

GET THE COMPLETE
Guerrilla Arsenal!

Guerrilla Marketing: Secrets for Making Big Profits from Your Small Business, Third Edition   ISBN 0-395-90625-3

The book that started the Guerrilla Marketing revolution is now updated and expanded. Called "the Bible of lively, low-cost marketing tips" by the *Los Angeles Times,* it's full of the latest strategies, information on the hottest technologies, details about the fastest growing markets, and management lessons for the twenty-first century.

Guerrilla Marketing Online: The Entrepreneur's Guide to Earning Profits on the Internet, Second Edition
ISBN 0-395-86061-X

Basic training for survival and success online from Jay Levinson and computer book author Charles Rubin. From building and maintaining a Web site to creating an online catalog and encouraging users to shop on the net, this will turn entrepreneurs into Internet marketing experts.

Guerrilla Marketing Online Weapons   ISBN 0-395-77019-X

This book offers one hundred low-cost, high-impact tools and techniques that will help businesses take advantage of the Internet's tremendous marketing potential. From e-mail addresses and signatures to storefronts, feedback mechanisms, electronic catalogs, and press kits, Levinson and Rubin's *Weapons* will help any business define, refine, and post its message online with ease.

The Guerrilla Marketing Handbook   ISBN 0-395-70013-2

An essential companion to *Guerrilla Marketing,* this practical guide offers thousands of contacts, ideas, and examples that will help transform plans into specific actions, turning any business into a marketing powerhouse.

Guerrilla Financing: Alternative Techniques to Finance Any Small Business ISBN 0-395-52264-1

This is the ultimate sourcebook for anyone who needs capital for a business venture, even if they have run out of money and been turned down by the bank. *Guerrilla Financing* is the first book to describe in detail the many traditional and alternative sources of funding available for small and medium-size businesses.

Guerrilla Marketing Attack: New Strategies, Tactics, and Weapons for Winning Big Profits ISBN 0-395-50220-9

This sequel to *Guerrilla Marketing* is a directive for planning, launching, and maintaining an all-out marketing offensive for the long haul. *Guerrilla Marketing Attack* explains how to avoid running out of fuel by maximizing limited start-up resources and turning prospects into customers, investments into profits.

Guerrilla Marketing Excellence: The Fifty Golden Rules for Small-Business Success ISBN 0-395-60844-9

Outlining fifty basic truths that can make or break a company, *Guerrilla Marketing Excellence* takes readers beyond do-it-yourself marketing guides, explaining not just how to market, but how to market with excellence.

Guerrilla Selling: Unconventional Weapons and Tactics for Increasing Your Sales ISBN 0-395-57820-5

Today's increasingly competitive business environment requires new and progressive skills and commitment from sales staffs. *Guerrilla Selling* presents unconventional selling tactics and practical tips that are essential for success.

Guerrilla Advertising: Cost-Effective Tactics for Small-Business Success ISBN 0-395-68718-7

Jay Levinson applies his proven guerrilla philosophy to advertising. Full of anecdotes about past and current advertising successes and failures, this book entertains as it teaches the nuts and bolts of advertising for small businesses.

Guerrilla Marketing for the Home-Based Business
ISBN 0-395-74283-8

Typically undercapitalized and short on relevant marketing know-how, home-based businesses have specific marketing needs. Using case studies, anecdotes, illustrations, and examples, guerrilla marketing gurus Jay Levinson and Seth Godin present practical, accessible, and inspirational marketing advice for America's fastest-growing business segment.

The Way of the Guerrilla ISBN 0-395-92478-2

An invaluable blueprint for future business success, *The Way of the Guerrilla* includes advice for both new and seasoned entrepreneurs on everything from preparing a focused mission statement and hiring responsible employees to finding more time for family and the community and sustaining one's passion for work. Enlightened and successful entrepreneurs will discover that a balanced life is the means to achieving emotional and financial success.